ROADMAPS

TO VALUE-BASED

PROFITABILITY

A Practice Transformation Guide

Jennifer Ternay

MGMA
Medical Group Management Association®

ROADMAPS

TO VALUE-BASED

PROFITABILITY

A Practice Transformation Guide

Jennifer Ternay

Published By: MGMA
Production / Partner Publisher: EGZ Publications

Summary: "This book offers tools and techniques to help medical practice administrators create plans to maximize profit under value-based systems—current with today's delivery system and that optimizes provider productivity and efficiency, practice profitability, staff recruitment and retention, and patient value."-- Provided by publisher.

ISBN: 978-1-56829-669-2
Medicine--Practice. 2. Medical offices--Management.
I. Medical Group Management Association. II. Title.
[DNLM: 1. Practice Management, Medical. W 80]

Item 1007
ISBN: 978-1-56829-669-2

Published in Centennial, Colorado
Medical Group Management Association
Printed in the United States of America   10 9 8 7 6 5 4 3 2 1

Table of Contents

Book Overview

Value-based care is happening. It is the direction the industry is moving, and embracing it early is the difference between sinking or swimming. This book provides a roadmap to navigating a complex landscape that will allow your practice to flourish where others will fail. It provides information regarding aspects of your practice that need to be evaluated, including key elements to incorporate into your daily workflows and overall operations.

Chapters 1 and 2 address the strategy of your practice. Rather than making value-based reimbursement payments the primary focus of how your practice adapts, the early material walks through an overview of why the industry is shifting to value-based reimbursement. The book then covers an initial assessment of your practice in terms of mission and values, the patients you serve, internal staff roles and responsibilities, and your external positioning in the healthcare space. Adopting a value-based approach to delivery of care requires a fundamental shift in how your practice operates. Changing infrastructure takes time but is not as complicated as changing how people act and behave. To be able to deliver and demonstrate improved health outcomes necessitates a cultural shift.

This cultural shift involves increasing awareness and understanding about what is changing and why the change is needed. Working to change the culture in any organization requires discipline and dedication, and most people are resistant to change. With value-based care, your approach requires change in both your staff and your patients. Understanding how to work through this process is described in Chapter 3.

The next section of the book walks you through understanding the patients you serve—and the local community. In moving from a fee-for-service (FFS) based practice toward a patient-centered approach to care, your practice must align resources to help improve the health and well-being of your patients. This orientation toward patient-centeredness goes beyond resolving acute needs. The focus is on identifying individuals that need additional assistance and holistically considering them. You look beyond the presenting problem to assess and incorporate knowledge about social determinants of health, cultural competencies, and behavioral health.

The book continues to define—in greater detail—how to structure your practice infrastructure and staffing. It outlines how to promote better outcomes through patient access to care. Some topics covered include:

- utilizing evidence-based care with a comprehensive assessment and reconciliation of medications during patient visits,
- using practice resources to assist in the delivery of care, and
- maximizing existing staff capabilities and talents.

In Chapter 8, the book provides information about developing and maintaining team-based care. Across the country, the number of practices experiencing workforce shortages and burnout is increasing. Embedding team-based care within your practice helps minimize the effects of these two growing problems. Furthermore, under a value-based care model, patients must identify their needs and preferences as well as participate in care. Engagement and activation of patients are integral to success and improved outcomes.

Later chapters provide a view of additional supports and tools for patients to assist in delivering a better patient experience and increasing patient satisfaction. Chapter 11 covers the move into value-based reimbursement and payer support for potential restructuring of your practice. Understanding how to make a compelling business case will help your practice negotiate favorable terms and ease the financial outlay associated with the transition to value-based care.

Lastly, the long-term survival of a practice depends on maintaining the transformation to delivering value-based care. This requires a focus on continuous quality improvement. The final chapter is designed to assist any practice in tracking results and embedding continuous quality improvement.

CHAPTER 1

Getting Ahead of the Curve

Healthcare faces challenges driven by workforce shortages, technology, consumerism, and escalating treatment costs. Patients are not engaged in treatment, yet the push toward value-based payments requires healthcare practices to be accountable for results. To succeed in healthcare where reimbursement is tied to outcomes, lowering costs, and improving the patient experience, every healthcare organization must embrace the concept of value-based care, which is focused on the patient. Value-based care requires the practice be structured around meeting the needs of patients, giving them the tools to manage their own care. Each patient will have unique needs and managing health encompasses a wide spectrum from prevention of illness to living with chronic illness to end stages of life.

The current system tends to address illness after it occurs rather than focusing on prevention and education. It is a challenging calculation that 50% of all healthcare costs are driven by 5% of the population.[1] The presence of multiple chronic conditions leads to fragmented care when services are not coordinated. Patients lack knowledge to manage their conditions or navigate the healthcare system. Practices are facing competing demands. New ways of delivering care may not seem an immediate requirement. Being ready to adapt to new payment mechanisms requires lead time to shift the way your practice functions and the ability to demonstrate outcomes with data. This means preparing for changes now so that you are ready in 12 to 24 months.

The US Federal Government has stepped in, pushing for change through regulation and mandating contractual requirements for participation in Medicare and Medicaid programs, affecting both providers and health plans. Why? Attempts to address the issues of the industry are disparate, with many parties proposing ideas on how to fix the growing problems. But segments of the healthcare industry ignore or disregard the proposed fixes, dismissing them to be the latest flavor of punch. When the majority sit back and take no action, regulation tends to result, forcing change.

Regulatory change is forcing healthcare to move from volume of services (with FFS billing) to demonstrating value in terms of better health outcomes, lower costs, and improved population health. As an industry, many parties are trying to figure out how to change the delivery of care and engage patients. We are sitting at the intersection of population health, patient-centered care, and health outcomes, seeking the best way to move forward on the road to improving overall health while lowering the cost of healthcare.

How We Arrived at the Healthcare Intersection

Over the last decade, four major pieces of legislation have been enacted that altered payments for providers:

- Medicare Improvements for Patients and Providers Act (MIPPA) in 2008
- Affordable Care Act (ACA) in 2010
- Protecting Access to Medicare Act (PAMA) in 2014
- The Medicare Access and CHIP Reauthorization Act of 2015 (MACRA)

Each act has changed the landscape of reimbursement and, while there is a significant amount of debate over the future of MACRA, value-based reimbursement is not going away.[2] Health plans in managed Medicare and Medicaid markets are contractually required to demonstrate mandated levels of payments using value-based methodology. But what *is* value-based care?

The Value-Based Care Healthcare Delivery Model

Value-based care is a healthcare delivery model that pays for improving patient and population health outcomes. In 2001, the Institute of Medicine (now the National Academy of Medicine) issued the report, *Crossing the Quality Chasm: A New Health System for the 21st Century*, which identified immense gaps between good healthcare and what people experience.[3] The report identified six aims for healthcare delivery:

- Safe
- Effective
- Patient-centered
- Timely
- Efficient
- Equitable

This report highlighted the issues within healthcare and created intense focus on looking at how to improve it. The impact of this report has continued over the last two decades to shift attention on how to close the gaps. Since that time, the Institute for Healthcare Improvement (IHI) created a framework to optimize health performance. Introduced in 2007, the framework is based on three core goals, known as the IHI Triple Aim. The goals are:

1. Make care better for individuals (quality and satisfaction).
2. Improve population health.
3. Reduce per capita costs.[4]

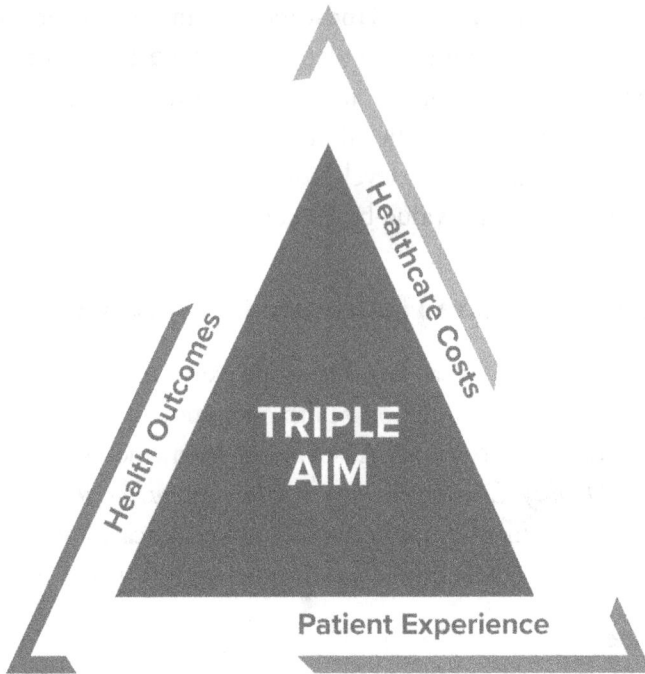

FIGURE 1.1   Triple Aim

It has been proposed to expand these three dimensions to address a fourth component that focuses on taking care of those that deliver care or play supporting roles.[5] Some organizations have independently taken the Triple Aim and added a fourth dimension important for their own strategies, calling their endeavors the Quadruple Aim.[6]

With the shifting focus on how healthcare is delivered and the promotion of value-based payment methodologies, the Department of Health and Human Services (HHS) through the Centers for Medicare & Medicaid Services (CMS) created the Health Care Payment Learning and Action Network (LAN) in March 2015. The LAN is a forum for sharing information about developing Advanced Alternative Payment Models (APMs) that support payment for delivering value, as defined below. As part of this work, the LAN produced a framework for defining APMs to allow for conversation using the same common definitions. The framework defines the following categories:

- Category 1
  - ○ fee-for-service payment with no link to quality and value
- Category 2
  - ○ fee-for-service with a link of payment to quality and value
- Category 3
  - ○ APMs built on fee-for-service architecture
- Category 4
  - ○ population-based payment

Many of the initial efforts to introduce value-based payments have been to move providers to Category 2 payments. Shifting to Categories 3 and 4 will require a broader focus on population health, promoting more than the quality measures associated with process measures, and ultimately taking financial risk. There will be more about this in Chapter 2.

Many programs have been initiated to build strength and capacity in value-based delivery of care. Not only are health plans supporting programs like the patient centered medical home (PCMH) and bundled payments, but federal and state initiatives have also been established. Here is a sampling of some of the programs that are encouraging implementation of the value-based care:

- Primary care transformation at the state level, like the New York DSRIP[7]
- SAMHSA grants to implement CCBHC for behavioral health[8]
- The CMS Innovation Center oncology care model[9]
- The CMS Innovation Center's ACO programs[10]
- Bundled episode-of-care payment initiatives, like the BPCI Initiative[11]
- MACRA: MIPS and APMs[12]

While there are specific programs designed to encourage participation, there is still opportunity to craft a program that meets your needs as a provider and those of your payers.

Population Health and Patient-Centered Care

A larger goal of the Triple Aim is not only to improve the lives of patients as individuals, but to also create positive change in entire populations. With a focus on education and support, improving the health of one individual can ripple to affect the lives of those around the individual. Continuing to spread through contact with others, the effect ultimately impacts the community as a whole. Using population health management strategies and stratifying patients based on need can allow your practice to structure resources and provide support based on identifying individuals at risk of developing chronic conditions, or those individuals that need a greater level of assistance in attaining the full capability of self-management. Within the context of population health, evidence-based guidelines and clinical best practices are to guide decisions about care, with care-planning being individualized to meet the needs and preferences of the patient.

The goal of value-based care is to foster a healthcare system that places the patient at the center of all decisions and encourages coordinated care. Coordinated care flows across the continuum of services with a focus on the person, not just a specific condition or acute need. Approaching care based on each patient's level of understanding and engagement allows for customization within the broader context of population health. To progress, we need to merge the concepts of population health, patient-centered care, and improved quality of life through better health and wellness into one seamless road of coordinated care.

Values and the Value-Based Future

Successful companies use organizational values to shape how they do business. The gold standard for customer service is represented by organizations like Disney and Ritz Carlton.[13] These companies are fueled by a focus on the customer. Healthcare is long overdue for shifting the focus to the patients served and their caregivers.

Burdened by a complex system of regulations and risk management with misaligned payment systems, healthcare has fostered an environment of generating revenue. At times the focus on revenue disregards whether the recommended care is truly needed, or if it is being ordered to cover legal risk. In certain situations, providers are forced to follow certain protocols to prove that more advanced testing is needed to meet health plan requirements. The current healthcare system also provides perverse incentives that generate financial rewards for billing more services. Potential malpractice lawsuits also drive the push to perform tests and procedures—just to be safe—despite the risk of an adverse outcome being low.

FOUNDATION OF VALUE-BASED CARE

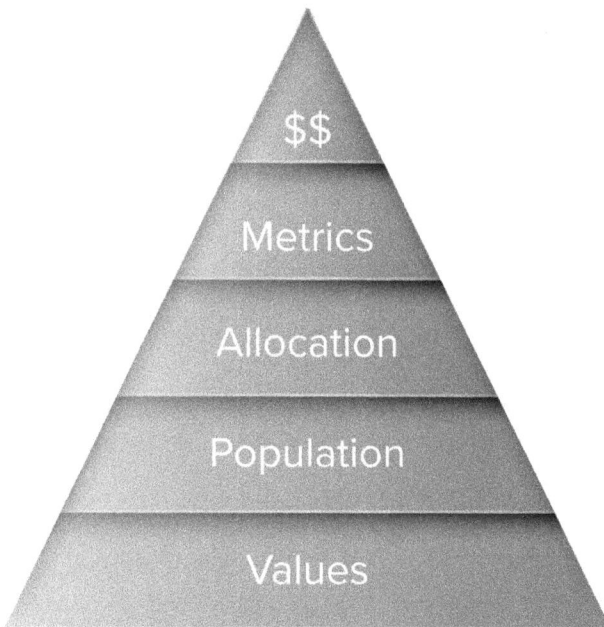

FIGURE 1.2   Foundation of Value-Based Care

Providers care about their patients and can find rules constraining and experience frustration when certain elements are outside of their control. Deciding how to work within the constraints of the reimbursement system reflects your organizational values. Value statements are made every day with ordinary actions, expressed everywhere whether consciously or unconsciously. Using values to mindfully drive business generates a competitive advantage both in delivering on patient needs and wants as well as retaining staff and creating a positive work environment.

Value-based payment methodologies are an attempt to fix an ever-growing problem. Using financial mechanisms and incentives, the goal is to create incentives for change. The intention of value-based care is to move the industry in the right direction, towards focusing on the patient individually as well as the entire patient population. To succeed in value-based care, practices need to adapt how they think and act, placing the patient at the center of everything, while simultaneously demonstrating effectiveness. This means sharpening or learning new skills and changing how you view your role. [14]

CHAPTER 2

First Steps to Making
Change Meaningful and Achievable

Maybe your practice is exploring options to enter the world of value-based care as a way of generating new revenue streams. Or maybe your practice is looking to gain a competitive advantage, or even just to stay in the game…but can you really make any type of meaningful change and keep the lights on? You can—by making the changes meaningful so that staff and patients are logically and emotionally involved. The logical explanations appeal to the brain and address whether the person can support the change: Does it make sense? The emotional commitment comes from appealing to a person's core values and sense of purpose: Does it feel right?

As health plans and other payers continue to adopt payment models that require demonstration of value and quality, transforming how you deliver care allows your practice to compete. The starting point for this transformation is understanding who you serve—their needs—and then assessing your internal structures, processes, and people. External influences also must be considered. As you evaluate your internal capabilities, utilizing your strengths is a good starting point for determining what outcomes will be easier to achieve. To move forward with this assessment, a gap analysis is created between what you have today and what you need to create to deliver value-based care. The gap analysis allows you to evaluate options to determine if resources are available to promote the transition.

Your overall approach needs to focus on answering these questions:

- What is the status of your organization today?
- How does your current status compare to where you need to be to capitalize on your strengths to demonstrate outcomes that matter in value-based care?
- What matters to your stakeholders, e.g., owners, patients, payers?
- What are the steps you need to take to get to the end goal?

In moving forward with transforming your practice, you will need to address identified gaps. Closing gaps and reinforcing strengths guides your transformation.

Who Do You Serve?

The starting point before beginning an assessment of your strengths and weaknesses is to clarify who you serve. While this may seem to have an obvious answer, consider a three-part approach to defining this. The three components are:

- Mission and vision
- Patients you currently serve
- Local community (from a population health perspective)

Whether a solo provider, a small partnership, a multi-specialty practice, or a health system, all practices are created with a focus which is defined in their mission and/or vision statements. This mission drives the purpose of the organization. As a business, your mission and vision also define who you serve, how you serve, and what your values are. The goal of these statements is to create a unified direction for your practice.

Nonprofit practices or organizations are mission driven. An example is a Federally Qualified Health Center (FQHC) that provides healthcare to individuals that are indigent, underinsured, or otherwise limited in access to care. Behavioral health organizations and practices are often also nonprofit, with missions dedicated to serving individuals living with serious mental illness, substance use disorders, and intellectual disabilities. **When considering outcomes that create meaning for the practice, alignment with the mission is critical.**

If your practice does not have formal mission and vision statements, take the time to create them as part of this process. When your mission and vision are used as your guiding principles, decisions can be simplified by weighing the options against them. The mission, vision, and values of a practice are foundational to keep staff engaged and are essential to rally them toward meeting and exceeding their goals. When your practice operates out of alignment with these statements, your mission, vision, and values become meaningless and viewed as hypocritical. People care about the goals of the organization. Having strongly stated principles can differentiate your practice in the marketplace and help with hiring and retaining staff.

Only 52% of polled MGMA members were satisfied with their organizations' cultures, i.e., norms, values, and mission.[1] Be sure to start with examining both the written documentation and the reality of day-to-day behavior. Don't be afraid to talk to your staff and ask them about how they view the practice. By connecting the desired outcomes to your mission, you create a measuring tape for what outcomes make sense to pursue, while fostering staff engagement.

Mission and vision as a recruitment strategy: hiring individuals that demonstrate core values strengthens your practice and creates reinforcement and consistency. Make sure to use this principle when crafting your recruitment campaigns and hiring process.

Consider not only the people the practice currently serves but also individuals in the surrounding communities and those that you may want to bring into your practice. How do you accomplish this? Examine your patients across many characteristics, including common conditions treated, and compare them to those prevalent in the community. Although the top diagnosed medical conditions in adults are generally hypertension, diabetes, hyperlipidemia, and coronary heart disease, understanding other factors such as comorbidities and social determinants of health allows for further definition of the needed services and desired outcomes.[2] Taking into account comorbidities and social determinants of health develops outcomes with greater impact for your patients, creating the desired ripple effect within the community (see Chapter 4).

As a competitive strategy, your practice may focus on health disparities based on your existing patients or address a larger need within the community. Addressing these needs can develop expertise and create a specialization for your practice. For example, if you are a primary care practice that sees a significant number of patients with asthma, you may want to focus on outcomes associated with the condition of asthma. Your reputation can extend to specializing in asthmatic patients while remaining within the scope of primary care. Being able to demonstrate good asthma control and the ability to treat patients effectively within primary care can create stronger relationships with payers, patients, and other medical professionals. An allergist or pulmonologist will understand that patients that are referred outside of your practice have a level of complexity that requires specialty care. This allows the specialist to focus on more intensive cases, easing issues with access and availability of specialty care.

On the flipside, if you are a stronger specialty practice, you can strengthen your clinical reputation for addressing complex cases and avoid losing scheduling availability to patients that should be served in primary care. Chapters 4 to 6 cover analysis of your patient population in further detail. Use the information gathered from your analysis of your patients to determine which outcomes make the most sense for your practice to demonstrate value-based care.

After assessing the characteristics of your patients and the local community, the next step in the assessment is to evaluate your practice in terms of your people, processes, and infrastructure.

Internal Readiness Assessment

Understanding your internal capabilities is essential to starting the journey to success in value-based care. Every organization, whether a solo practice, group practice, health system, or facility, needs to have a clear picture of its strengths and weaknesses. When assessing internal capabilities, there are several key areas to review.

- Culture
- Leadership and governance
- Staff
- Clinical practices
- Patient-centered care
- Technology
- Performance measurement and quality improvement
- Financial monitoring and funding
- Communication

During this process, you may find opportunities to further refine your target market, find new patients, and serve the larger community more effectively. This transformative process can allow your practice to be proactive in attracting certain types of patients rather than reactive to whoever shows up.

This list of recommendations for what to review may seem a bit daunting when starting out. Gaining an understanding of your organization will take time. The more thorough your assessment, the better understanding you will develop. In performing the assessment, you must decide where to focus your efforts based on the goals of the practice. Completing a top-to-bottom and sideways assessment may be difficult depending on the resources you have available, but the deeper

INTERNAL ASSESSMENT

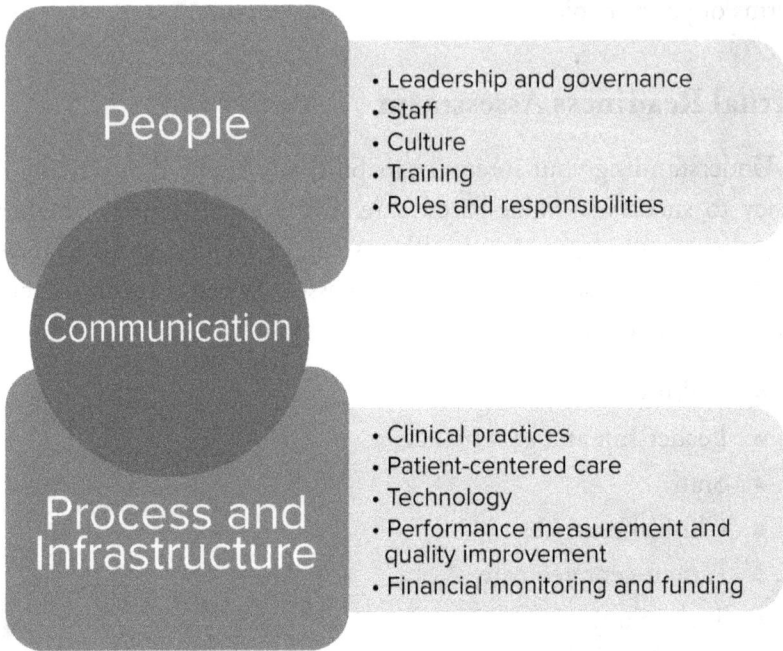

People

Communication

Process and Infrastructure

- Leadership and governance
- Staff
- Culture
- Training
- Roles and responsibilities

- Clinical practices
- Patient-centered care
- Technology
- Performance measurement and quality improvement
- Financial monitoring and funding

FIGURE 2.1   Internal Assessment

you go, the greater the potential reward from the information gathered. As you look at the gaps in your organization, you may find that focusing on one area at a time is easier to manage.

This readiness assessment should be completed by more than one individual. Selecting individuals with differing levels and roles will provide a better picture of your practice. A recommended approach is to complete individual assessments, then combine the results based on a consensus process. Gaining consensus involves discussing the difference in the individual scores and coming to agreement on a collective score. This process allows for dialogue and may reveal additional areas requiring improvement.

Look at specific functions and aspects of your practice on a continuum. Consider the evaluation responses on a scale, leveled 1 to 5, with 1 being the lowest (assessed item is completely missing) to 5 being the highest (everything is fully in place and functioning well). When examining each aspect of the evaluation, consider the availability of written documentation like policies and procedures, formal documents like job descriptions and performance evaluation, as well as reports and other monitoring tools. When reviewing the sections related to internal assessment, the following scoring definition is an example of how to determine your level of readiness when considering process.

1 – Absent
   o Evaluation item is not being done; barriers to completing this item exist and/or this has not been considered and does not exist; data is not available, or it may not be possible to document; level of awareness/knowledge is lacking; support is missing.

2 – Requires implementation
   o Basic understanding of what needs to be done, there is no formal process, but one could be put in place; data could be captured but currently is not; level of awareness/knowledge/acceptance is minimal; support is limited.

3 – Requires significant improvement
   o Evaluation item may exist; there may be a process, but it is neither documented nor tracked; documentation is captured but not used, written materials to support evaluation do not exist; some level of awareness, knowledge, or acceptance. Support exists, but skills need to be developed.

4 – Requires some improvement
   o Process is documented but may not be followed, report is available but not fully utilized; awareness/knowledge are present; some skills are demonstrated but require improvement.

15

5 – Functioning well
  ○ Process is documented in writing and is followed; monitoring of performance occurs through reports or other mechanisms; written materials to support evaluation item exist and are shared; awareness, skills, acceptance, and support are present; strong sense of objective.

For less tangible items, such as whether the culture and staff support value-based care, consider the level of awareness, knowledge, skills, acceptance, and support with the scale indicating the level of support from low to high. Remember, the internal environment is reviewed in terms of people, processes, and infrastructure.

People

When evaluating the readiness of the people involved in the organization to adopt and maintain a value-based care environment, all levels of staff should be involved. Each person needs to understand how he or she plays a role in delivering value and improving the lives of people served by the practice. Understanding and directing the behaviors, motivations, and values of your staff is one of the most challenging aspects of any business. Developing soft skills for managing the culture, engaging staff, demonstrating leadership, and gaining support from the executive or governance structure is imperative to transform a practice from a mere organization into a high-performing entity that delivers value and quality while balancing the wise use of practice resources.

Culture

The power and influence of culture cannot be emphasized enough. Culture is the shared assumptions, values, and beliefs that define how people behave in the workplace. As a major driving force in any business, culture assists in or detracts from achieving your organizational goals. To deliver quality and value, your culture must support these objectives.

In assessing your readiness to adopt value-based care, an evaluation of the culture of your practice needs to occur. Depending on the size of your practice or organization, culture may vary across departments, locations, and level of staff. The culture needs to support the concept that care is:

- Patient-Centered
- Team-Based
- Comprehensive
- Coordinated
- Integrated
- Accessible
- Valuable

To assess the culture of your organization, a review of both written materials and observations of your staff and patients provide essential insights. The best way to gather this information is through surveys, focus groups, and direct interaction. Examples for gathering staff insights include climate surveys or staff satisfaction surveys.

Most practices are already surveying patients. Your patient satisfaction surveys provide indirect answers about the values of your organization if the questions are worded to address specific topics like access, customer service, value, coordination, etc. Consider your satisfaction scores from the patient perspective when evaluating the culture of your practice. In areas where your patient satisfaction scores are lower, your assessment score would be rated lower. Make sure your surveys include questions that capture the characteristics listed above.

Leadership and Governance

Without support from your practice's leaders and—where applicable—your governing body, transforming how you deliver care is not possible. The leadership must fully back the changes, as the transformation process requires dedicated resources, funding, and moral support. The process takes time, and a focus on the required changes must be an organizational priority. How your practice or organization is legally structured can cover a wide variety of options, like sole proprietorships, partnerships with two or more partners, corporations with a large executive management team, a formal board of directors, or an independent practice association (IPA). In all cases, the top levels of the organization need to understand, believe in, and support value-based care. Collectively, your leadership and governing body must allocate enough resources to support the transition process and maintain the commitment on an ongoing basis, or your practice risks wasting time and resources.

Additionally, an executive champion should be identified among your leadership to spearhead the transformation process. As will be discussed in Chapter 3, the role of executive champion is essential to managing change.

Staff

When evaluating the readiness of your organization to change, your assessment should examine the engagement and performance of your staff. Is your staff excited to be at work every day? Do they feel like they are making a difference? Or are they just there to get through the day and get out of the office as soon as possible? A successful transition will include engaging the staff and bringing them along in the process. The more engaged the staff are when on the clock the more excited they will be about a change that makes a healthier patient population while ensuring the financial well-being of the practice.

Both positive and negative factors influence employee engagement, such as the ability to grow, recognition of efforts and accomplishments, failure to challenge people creatively and intellectually, and whether work has meaning.[3]

In assessing current staff readiness, the goal is to look at the structure of positions and determine whether the staff are performing as expected. If they are not, shoring up weaker elements exposed by the assessment will help enhance performance. A combination of

> In moving to new ways of delivering care, your practice requires job descriptions that reflect new roles and responsibilities. **Make sure you use job descriptions that align with organizational values and goals.** Reinforce the job descriptions with a compensation system that promotes performance and offer training to introduce or strengthen skills. Design a performance evaluation program that promotes the desired traits and behaviors and rewards for delivering based on the job descriptions. Robust job descriptions aligned compensation systems, supportive training, and correlated performance evaluations are important tools for managing change.

many factors will influence the whole—however, starting small with incremental changes can shift the tide and create positive momentum to carry the transition to a successful conclusion.

Job descriptions are often considered a useless piece of paperwork required by someone in human resources or only needed when interviewing a prospective candidate. This perception could not be further from the truth. A job description, when used appropriately, is a powerful tool to engage staff and ensure that the goals and values of the organization are supported. If your practice does not use job descriptions or has descriptions that do not accurately capture how staff perform their jobs, you must get those into alignment before implementing change.

In evaluating job descriptions during the internal assessment, focus on incorporating the concepts of patient-centeredness, excellence in quality, high value, and teamwork. Additionally, each job description should clearly delineate tasks and functions that require individuals to work at the top of their license—or if unlicensed, still maximizing the full potential of the position. The goal is to delegate work to utilize the full scope of a person's capabilities.

Encouraging compliance with job descriptions happens through performance evaluations.[4] To make performance management systems effective, evaluations should establish accountability for results and offer recognition and rewards. Recognition and rewards are not just monetary. An example of a non-monetary reward is an employee of the month program. Your ability to navigate through the changes can be facilitated with a well-functioning performance management system that evaluates and compensates based on fulfillment of defined roles and responsibilities.

Training is a great way to expand skills, bring out people's creativity, and reinforce alignment with the goals and values of the organization. When evaluating readiness for change, understanding the capacity of the practice to incorporate a regular training plan that includes all staff is important—as is understanding what is currently in place. The training plan should include not only the basics required by HIPAA and other regulations, but also target new knowledge and skills needed to deliver value-based care (see Chapter 8). As an additional benefit, engaging staff through training also reduces turnover, which is a goal of most organizations.[5] While resources may limit the extent of available training, this is an important component for successful change and should be planned annually.

Process and Infrastructure

With process and infrastructure, your readiness evaluation needs to consider aspects of clinical practices, technology, performance measurement and quality improvement, financial monitoring, funding, and communication. As you evaluate your process and infrastructure, the stronger that you can rate your compliance with the stated ideal, the higher your organizational readiness for transforming to value-based care.

Clinical Practice

This part of the readiness assessment considers the degree to which your practice currently:

1. Evaluates and manages patient needs.
2. Uses evidence-based and best practices.

3. Handles cases that require care coordination.

4. Transitions between levels of care.

5. Promotes care management.

To ensure appropriate evaluation of patient needs, consider the completeness of the information your practice collects and documents during visits. Accurately assessing the level of understanding (literacy) of patients will assist both the practice and the patient in managing their needs.[6]

Value-based care should minimize discrepancies and errors among your providers. One of the ways to achieve this is by encouraging best practices, use of established medical protocols, and exercise of evidence-based medicine. It will only be possible to assess the adherence to these best practices if their use is documented, so ensure this becomes part of the practice's process. Your practice should ensure that all team members have full access to continually updated information about patient needs, preferences, and care. Capturing this information within the patient record facilitates communication among the team members and makes the process of sharing information with providers outside of your practice a little easier.

Evaluating the regular and consistent standardized clinical guidelines for the best care: When using evidence-based guidelines and best practices as your medical protocols, inappropriate services are minimized. Gaps in care are easier to identify when comparing current and historical care to the guidelines. While independent judgment is still to be exercised, the guidelines and practices are intended to help providers make the best decisions for specific conditions.

The next component of assessing clinical care is the level of coordination with other providers and facilities. When coordination is not consistent and thorough, patients can fall through the cracks. Care coordination should take a 360° approach, with clear communication among all involved parties, including the patient. An often-overlooked factor is if the patient has a primary provider and circumstances cause the patient's primary provider to change. The primary provider may change as the complexity of the condition and associated treatments adjust. Regular updates save time and money for all providers involved and are better for the patient's overall health and care plan.

In reviewing the improvement opportunities for your organization, assess the level of coordination for referrals, labs, images, and testing. This coordination includes providing referrals or prescriptions, tracking whether results are received, and ensuring patients are notified of the normal and abnormal results of tests, images, and labs. For referrals, evaluate if the level of communication between the providers includes enough documentation to eliminate redundant treatment and procedures. Also, assess if referrals and coordination include the exchange of a complete medical history and identify how the patient will be managed among more than one provider.

For coordination with facilities, the final goal is to ensure that communication occurs when a patient is admitted to the emergency room or inpatient unit, regardless of whether the admission is planned or unplanned. Your practice assessment of current processes should review communications regarding admissions and identify the level of documentation and information being shared while the patient is at the hospital and at the time of discharge. The practice should be proactively contacting patients to ensure that a follow-up visit occurs shortly after discharge and that discharge summaries are obtained. This will be discussed further in Chapter 5.

Patient-Centered

To achieve improved health outcomes, patients must be encouraged to actively participate in their health and well-being and be supported by your practice. This type of patient-centered approach can present a host of challenges given the variety of influences on patient behavior. When assessing the ability to influence outcomes, evaluate your practice in terms of the current level of participation and interaction with patients. Certain elements can assist with engaging patients and ensure that the voice of the patient in included in practice operations. Having multiple modes for feedback offers the ability for the practice to understand patient concerns and needs. This can include:

- Patient and family advisory councils
- Patient satisfaction surveys
- Comment boxes

Patient and Family Advisory Councils: Patient and Family Advisory Councils (PFACs) or Patient Advisory Councils (PACs) are a promising new approach to gain patient input to help the medical practice. A report in the American Academy of Family Physicians; (AAFP) *FPM* magazine entitled "Patient Advisory Councils: Giving Patients a Seat at the Table" offers success stories some practices are having with the model. The report also has recommendations on best practices.

Being ready to implement and utilize these tools helps indicate the practice's level of readiness. Additionally, the evaluation of current processes should assess the needs associated with health literacy, language, and cultural influences. This can include providing written communication as well as oral communication. Actively engaging a patient takes the whole office. The provider, the care team, and the office team must establish trust through a relationship that considers the totality of the patient's needs. This will go beyond the patient's medical needs to also include cultural, linguistic, social, behavioral, and literacy needs.

Being patient-centered means involving the patient, and, as appropriate, caregivers in care planning and developing shared goals based on their needs and preferences. The ability to create shared goals is a key aspect to address.

The final piece is to tie together the insights you have gathered and evaluate how well your practice supports self-management, shared decision making, and patient education.

Technology

Within your practice, technology should make workflows and processes easier. The currently available electronic health record systems (EHRs) tend to have issues in this area. When assessing technology, review not only the EHR but also include a review of any other technology used within your practice. When assessing technology, consider functional aspects, ease of use, and whether the technology facilitates the delivery of quality care. The experience and perception of electronic records has been largely negative, but to demonstrate outcomes, documentation must be collected and analyzed. Your EHR should not create unnecessary administrative burden. Otherwise, your processes will need to be altered to work around inefficiencies created by the EHR so that data is collected. Without data, the evidence of improvement in health and well-being is theoretical. As with the development of medical guidelines, evidence is compelling, and it is data that provides the evidence the practice is improving health or achieving outcomes.

In assessing the usefulness of your EHR, the first requirement is that the system is certified by ONC-ATCB.[7] Ideally, the EHR should be configured to assist the workflow process, although this has been a significant challenge for existing systems. If workflow problems arise (or already exist) while using the EHR, evaluate if the gap in readiness can be resolved by altering the EHR, updating templates, or by providing different training to your staff to increase skills in working with the EHR. Also, assess the level of integration of the practice management and clinical modules.

Other functionality to assess within the EHR is the integration of a patient portal and ways to communicate with patients. The ability to schedule appointments, send appointment reminders, and share information with the patient are tools that assist in providing access and follow-up to improve patient outcomes.

Interfaces with other providers to share information electronically are critical. The ability to exchange relevant information in structured

The EHR total package: Review the EHR's ability to capture clinical documentation for elements that assist in gathering a complete picture of the patient. These elements include not only basics like vitals and demographics but also comprehensive health assessments, care plans, and coordinated data exchanges for medications, images, labs, and referrals. With care plans, the system should provide information on associated best practices or evidence-based guidelines as well as incorporate patient input. The EHR should capture patient preferences, barriers to care, how barriers are addressed as part of the care plan and assist with the documentation of the care plan. The patient should be able to leave with a copy of the care plan along with educational materials and any related tools specific to the condition, such as food journals or blood sugar logs for diabetics.

fields allows for data to be imported and exported without manual intervention. Of particular importance is to gather information in a timely manner regarding inpatient and emergency department admissions. While there may be legal and contractual issues to resolve to enact free-flowing data exchange, when assessing the practice's use of technology, evaluate the ability to automate the mutual sharing of information with important care partners.

Lastly, reporting is another technology function to assess. Data is only useful if it can be reported in a timely manner with actionable information. As discussed in the next section, performance measurement and review are needed to verify if you are on track for meeting your outcome goals. Your level of readiness not only to capture data but create meaningful reports that assist your practice to deliver higher levels of care must be evaluated. Your assessment should consider data collection, ease of generating data for analysis, and your ability to create goals and benchmark to external standards.

Performance Measurement and Quality Improvement

Developing performance measurement practices and quality improvement processes is critical in value-based care.[8] The quality improvement process requires performance measurement and management to achieve desired outcomes and demonstrate improvement in health. In evaluating readiness to engage in value-based care, performance metrics or outcomes must be used. Use quantitative and qualitative data, as well as other available sources of information, to determine how your practice should perform versus how it currently performs with the following four steps:

1. Use your current performance metrics as the baseline.
2. Set goals to achieve improved performance.
3. Extract data and review it regularly to determine if actions taken are positively impacting performance.
4. Use a process to review performance objectively.[9] (One must be built if your practice doesn't have this tool.)[10]

Analytical skills are needed to compare performance to goals and identify when corrections are needed. Your review will consider what exists for a quality improvement process, from goal creation through the cycle of monitoring and analyzing performance. This can be assessed based on:

- availability of people and resources,
- policies and procedures,
- reports and distribution of information, and
- evaluating how data can be used to inform change.

Incorporating a quality improvement council with patient involvement is a great way to include your patients and have an external review of your performance.[11] In evaluating your practice readiness, whether you currently have a formal performance measurement and quality improvement process should be considered, as well as the overall support of leadership and staff for these activities. Through this process, performance data should be shared at the individual provider level and practice level. Transparency with data is gaining traction in many high-performing medical practices as a performance motivator and driver.[12]

Patient satisfaction surveys are another source of data for performance measurement. Evaluating the sufficiency of the responses to patient satisfaction surveys (i.e., quantity) and the ability to aggregate the responses plays a factor in determining readiness. The use of these surveys can lead to insights on patient perceptions which can influence behaviors and impact trust in the practice. Your assessment considers your current use of data to gain insight about how your practice functions along with acting on that information to improve your performance.

Chapter 12 goes into considerable detail on how to implement the processes required for performance measurement and quality improvement.

Financial Monitoring and Funding

As your practice begins participating in value-based payment programs, the ability to monitor financial performance and tie back achievement of outcomes to costs and revenue becomes essential. As the level of risk within value-based payments increases, the ability to manage that financial risk is crucial to the success and financial health of the organization.

If you're interested in pursuing payment methodologies based on a population of patients, confirm the ability to determine your cost to deliver services at a per unit cost or attributed life basis. Be aware that existing costs may increase due to the project costs associated with implementing new workflows, staffing, and/or technology. This information needs to be evaluated for both the implementation and ongoing costs, along with the potential new or additional revenue for delivering high-value outcomes.

The costs and revenue should be analyzed using a cost-benefit analysis (CBA) or return on investment (ROI) model. Assess the ability to manage financial risk, particularly if there is downside risk with the alternative payments. New payments may need to be negotiated with a payer, which requires the ability to create a strong business proposal delivered with well-honed presentation and negotiation skills. The more data you have that supports your negotiating position the better.

As part of evaluating financial functions, assess not only capability for analysis and monitoring but also actual resources. The transformation process could involve an upfront, initial investment to transition the underlying delivery of care. This investment can involve expenses related to personnel, technology, training, and external consulting. The degree of your readiness involves understanding current financial resources as well as projected sources of funds.

Budgeting for anticipated expense and revenue and understanding how to pay for the transition phase are the lynchpins to a successful transition to (or growth of) a value-based care practice. Also review your capability to track and monitor actual financial performance with projections. Capability includes producing information in a timely manner and with related analysis.

Communication

During any change, communication becomes even more critical. The ability to keep your staff and patients informed and engaged will determine the speed and long-term success of the transformation of your practice.

Communication mechanisms (with both staff and patients) associated with changes are to be assessed in terms of:

- Frequency
- Effectiveness
- Method

For internal communications, consideration should be given to increasing the use of regular meetings across the practice and within clinical teams. Quick touch-base meetings to review patients scheduled for the day will assist with preplanning and identifying any concerns or missing tests, images, labs, or consultations. Practice meetings that include all staff are a great way to keep everyone informed about results associated with outcomes. It will also provide a forum for discussing ideas and resolving any barriers.

When assessing communications with your patients, review the types of information that are currently shared and what additional needs could be met by additional communication. Your patients will need to understand how value-based care changes the traditional delivery of care by increasing their involvement in decision-making and expecting that they engage more actively in improving their health. To assist in this patient education, materials need to be available at the appropriate reading level and translated into other languages as needed.

Solid communication helps empower everyone involved in a value-based care practice. In this case, better communication is, quite literally, healthy.

External Readiness Assessment

An assessment of external influences, including payers, competitors, and regulatory requirements, will highlight the practice's opportunities and threats as the practice tries to understand its readiness to adopt value-based payment models. A tool to implement this is a strengths, weaknesses, opportunities, and threats (SWOT) Analysis in Porter's Five Forces Model.[13]

Payers

A major influencing factor in the ability to be successful in value-based care is the relationship with payers. Since the payer is the party making the value-based payments, the outcomes need to align with payer goals. In assessing the readiness for value-based care, an open and positive relationship with major payers is necessary.

Take the time to understand what, if any, interest the payers have in creating a new payment mechanism. Most payers are offering some level of value-based payments, but participation may be limited to certain providers and/or services. Understanding what is currently in place is good to evaluate, but the absence of a program applicable to your specific practice should not be a barrier to pursuing options. Your level of understanding the outcomes that are important to the payer creates the metric for readiness. Evaluate the ability of your practice to affect performance and influence those outcomes. A payer will be more interested in a proposal that helps with its costs and ability to demonstrate value and outcomes.

Competitors

What are your competitors doing? Demonstrating value through quality outcomes and efficient care can differentiate your practice in the market and the community. For some practices, obtaining independent accreditation or recognition has been leveraged for marketing value and quality. While independent certification is not necessary, being able to demonstrate concrete outcomes is always compelling to patients. More and more consumers of healthcare are evaluating their options by reviewing online ratings of providers before selecting where to seek care.

When comparing your practice to competitors, do not assess only against like types of practices. New types of indirect competition are coming from retail clinics and urgent care sites. For some patients, the convenience and ease of access may be appealing, and this may complicate your efforts to manage care and improve health outcomes. Indirect competition also comes from other high-performing organizations the patient interacts with, even those outside of healthcare. Patient experience is greatly influenced by the patient's perception of the practice, as well as by individual interactions. When you have a local business or another health practice or facility that excels in customer service, the bar is raised for all other businesses in the area. In gathering your readiness assessment, consider not just how the competitor performs, but also the influence of other types of organizations on your practice. You should assess not only your excellence in customer service but also the delivery of quality and value.

Regulatory

For providers participating in Medicare, the programs associated with MACRA are also drivers for transforming to value-based care. Under MIPS or APMs, depending on the size of the practice, providers earn points with higher reimbursement. As these programs evolve, value-based pay will only become more sophisticated. For providers that opt to absorb penalties rather than comply with requirements, the penalties become more significant over time. Additionally, there is a possibility that participation in Medicare could be limited (as has occurred with Medicaid). This could also apply to private insurers as they move to tighten networks by creating minimum requirements to participate in-network. Your assessment needs to consider regulatory pressure to adopt value-based payments.

Finalizing the Readiness Assessment

The results of assessing your internal strengths and weaknesses along with external opportunities and threats create required intelligence to determine how to move forward. Your assessment provides a baseline of where you are currently performing. This information, along with an understanding of quality measures and selecting appropriate measures, allows for further progress for planning your transformation.

Quality Measures

Quality measures are essential for tracking performance and provide a quantitative measure. The aim of the measure is to align with the National Academy of Medicine (formerly the Institutes of Medicine or IOM)-articulated goals that care be safe, effective, patient-centered, timely, efficient and equitable. A quality measure is the specific metric that assesses the result and determines if the goal has been met.

A good resource to understanding quality measures is the Agency for Healthcare Research and Quality's (AHRQ), which uses the industry standard Donabedian model quality measures that defines three categories:

- Structure
- Process
- Outcome[14]

As AHRQ describes on their website, structural measures "examine capacity, systems, and processes." An example they give of a structural measure is the ratio of physicians to patients.[15] Structural measures are used for accreditation or certification programs.[16]

Process measures reflect accepted clinical practices and assess actions taken by a provider to maintain or improve health. These process measures can be about general health or can be specific to a healthcare condition. The assumption with process measures is that the actions taken have a direct relationship to improving health. An example of a process measure is the rate of patients diagnosed with diabetes that have had a foot exam. According to AHRQ, "The majority of health care quality measures used for public reporting are process measures."[17]

The third category of quality measures in the Donabedian framework is outcome measures. An outcome measure describes the result of services or interventions. The outcome measure will generally reflect the effect on patient health, health status, or functioning. The measures tend to relate to mortality (death), morbidity (incidence of disease), and health-related quality of life. The challenge with outcome measures is determining the associated cause and effect. Because outcome measures tend to be broad in definition, multiple factors can influence the results. An example of an outcome measure is the rate of lower-extremity amputation among patients with diabetes.

A fourth category of measures associated with the patient experience is often promoted as a quality measure in addition to structural, process, and outcome measures.[18] Patient experience is primarily measured by patient satisfaction surveys. An example of a patient experience measure is, "How often did your personal doctor explain things in a way that was easy to understand?" This measure is not associated with a specific health outcome, but research has proven that positive patient experiences result in better engagement, stronger commitment to treatment plans, and being more receptive to medical advice.

When developing quality measures for value-based payment arrangements, one of the biggest challenges is determining measures that are acceptable to providers, especially in terms of being accountable for results. Much of the resistance around value-based payments centers around arguments that the provider cannot influence the outcome because so much is dependent upon the patient. This book will demonstrate that how your practice is structured, how providers interact with your patients, and how patients are encouraged to actively engage in care *are all* under your control. A coordinated practice effort in these areas can result in measurable outcomes. Committing to change and being willing to change are the biggest challenges. Accepting some level of risk for outcomes that may, on the surface, seem to be beyond your control can help with influencing changes in behavior when managed appropriately.

The personal outcome and patient experience are what matter most to your patients. Your process and structural measures help you achieve those outcomes with the patients. In the examples above, patients with diabetes will care more about the rate of amputation than the rate of foot exams. However, the process measure for foot exams measures adherence to a best practice that helps reduce the occurrence of amputation.

Sources of Measures

One resource for quality measures is the National Quality Forum (NQF). The NQF created a web-based tool called the Quality

Positioning System (QPS), which houses portfolios of quality measures.[19] There are over 1,000 measures available within the QPS, and measures can be filtered using multiple parameters such as the clinical condition, care setting, target population, etc. The measures are also identified by type of measure, including process, structure, outcome, as well as composite, cost/resource use, and efficiency. An example of a portfolio of measures is the 2016 Medicaid Adult Core Set, which shows twenty-two measures such as breast cancer screening and congestive heart failure rate. Measures are developed by multiple parties including government agencies, public and non-profit organizations, for-profit companies, and professional societies. Many measures are available in the public domain and can be tailored to meet the needs of your patient population and your practice. The challenge is to prioritize the most relevant measures.

Prioritizing Outcomes

As noted, the mission of the organization should be a driving factor in determining what outcomes are most meaningful. The mission of the organization reflects the reason for existence, desired outcome, and those served by your organization.

1. Your mission should tie to meeting the needs of the individuals you serve.
2. You should define and prioritize the types of quality measures using the information you have compiled on internal functions, external factors, and the needs of the patients being served.
3. The tasks need to be prioritized. The mission of the organization should be a key driver in determining whether focusing on a specific quality measure should be a priority.
4. If the quality measure does not support the mission of the organization, other measures should be given higher consideration.

As an example, if the mission of your practice is to support older patients covered by Medicare, you would not select measures associated only with children. In a similar manner, a specialty practice would not select measures that were not related to the conditions treated by the practice. While these are simple examples and may seem obvious, there may be times when the decisions are not as clear cut and the boundaries may be blurred. Going back to your mission can help with decision-making. Additionally, connecting the outcomes to your mission assists in gaining support, promoting consistency in communicating changes, and reinforcing an approach that is based on your values.

To gain a wide base of support and understand the true needs of the transformation to a value-based care practice, employees, patients, and other stakeholders should be involved in the process. Stakeholders can include parties like payers, owners, and advocates. Involving a broader group of individuals than those charged with managing and coordinating the actual transformation efforts allows for developing a broader perspective—and engages individuals in wanting the transformation to succeed.

Knowing the values and priorities of the employees, patients, and other stakeholders provides a richer set of criteria for identifying overall priorities. When prioritizing quality measures to implement, factors to consider are whether the measure is:

- Meaningful
  - Is it mission-oriented, clinically important and valid, related to values?
- Feasible
  - Can it be affordably implemented with available data?
- Actionable
  - Are benchmarks and standards available, and can the measures lead to clinical improvement?
- Purposeful
  - Is there internal or external demand from patients, payers, staff, and owners?

- Impactful
  - Is there is a potential payoff in terms of quality and financial reimbursement?

Below is an example of the scoring matrix for outcomes associated with diabetic care:

| Outcome Measure | Mission | Meaningful | | | Feasible (data/ resources/ process) | Actionable: benchmark or standard | Purposeful - demand | Pay-off in quality or $$ | Score |
		Value 1	Value 2	Value 3					
Weight	15	5	5	5	30	10	10	20	100
Rate of eye exams	3	3	3	3	2	5	2	5	3.2
Rate of foot exams	3	3	3	3	2	5	2	5	3.2
A1c <9	4	4	4	4	5	5	5	5	4.7
Rate of depression screening	3	3	3	3	4	5	5	5	4.1
Statin Use in Persons with Diabetes	3	3	3	3	3	5	3	3	3.2

TABLE 2.1   Scoring Matrix for Outcomes

The criteria are listed as column headings and assigned a weight based on the value assigned by your organization. In the above example, the highest-ranking factors are that the measure is meaningful (30) and feasible (30), followed by a payoff be present in terms of quality or financial reimbursement (20). Note that "meaningful" is further refined using organizational mission and the top three organizational values. While this level of detail can be skipped, having this additional definition may facilitate the decision-making. To be effective, your practice must clearly define "meaningful." For each outcome measure, a score of 1 to 5 is assigned to each of the criteria. A score of 5 means that that particular outcome has the largest impact on the criteria. The score in the last column is a weighted average based on the criteria weight (row labeled "Weight") and the score of 1 to 5 for each of the outcome measures. This total score creates an overall value that can be ranked. In the example above, measuring A1c scores has the greatest score and value. This evaluation tool can also be used to prioritize the overall approach to transformation as well as specific tasks.

The next phase is to combine the information from your readiness assessment and review of the most appropriate outcomes measures to create a plan for continuing to move forward. You have created a strong base understanding that allows for gaps to be identified between what you have in place currently and where you need to go. In some cases, you may find that you are tweaking certain functions to strengthen them; in other functions, you may need more work. The end goal is to create a vision of the future that drives accomplishment. Using tools and skills associated with project management and change management, you influence the actions, behaviors, and values of individuals within your practice or organization to achieve your vision.

Planning

As more and more pieces of the transformation roadmap come together, it becomes possible to plan actual change in a way that doesn't feel overwhelming. Gather the information from your overall assessment and determine the gaps between your current performance and where you want to be, or need to be, to participate in value-based care. In defining the future state of your practice, consider your strengths and the needs of your patient population. You will want to start out with small changes to build your confidence in both the ability to change and managing that change.

Identifying areas where you can capitalize on your strengths to demonstrate outcomes is best. Your assessment will also identify areas that need to be improved or developed in order to participate in value-based care. The planning stage involves brainstorming that uses all the available information. This information includes:

- the results of your assessment,
- available financial resources,
- patient needs and gaps in care,
- programs available to fund the transformation,
- an understanding of areas of interest to your major payers, and
- available outcome measures.

These gaps between what exists today and where you need to be should be converted into tasks within a project plan. What the changes are, and the timing of those changes, must be determined and prioritized. The process of pulling together your vision of the future precedes the development of your project plan, but understanding what needs to be accomplished, how long it will take, and what is realistic should all be considered before finalizing the picture of what your practice looks like under value-based care. More information about defining your vision (both how and why) is described in Chapter 3.

A key element of value-based care is measuring outcomes and demonstrating that your efforts result in improved health and well-being for your patients. In developing a roadmap to the future, a set of outcomes must be defined for measuring your performance, or you will get lost along the way. Measuring and monitoring these outcomes will let you know if you are progressing toward your goals or if correction is needed.

CHAPTER 3

Transforming Requires Leadership

You've tackled some of the most difficult parts of getting started—going from a blank slate to identifying areas of strength that help ease the transition and areas where improvements can be made. Changing the underlying functions of a practice requires significant energy and focus. After assessing the current culture and operations, the next step is to create a plan for what the new environment will look and feel like. Leadership will have to actively engage your staff. Shifting from one way of thinking and operating to a new way takes time. Encountering difficulties along the way should be expected. Having a plan for why the change is important and how the process will work assists with staying on track and not losing steam. Relating these changes back to the values of the practice is a great way to ensure that everyone sees how the transformation and change fit with what the practice stands for.

Many change models exist for working through transitions. While change involves altering workflows and processes, the most critical aspect of change will be the people. Understanding the difference and knowing how to address project planning—separate from the human relations of change management—facilitates transformation. If implementing value-based care only meant changing workflows, adding new technology, and working with data, the transition would be far easier. Understand that gaining acceptance and support from those impacted by the change is the most significant challenge. Within healthcare, there is significant complexity; this complicates the transition and, in many cases, requires that your practice incorporate new skills. Engaging members of your practice and even your patients to adapt to change is paramount. With the current pace of change, being nimble and able to adapt to new circumstances is important. Successful transformation takes a combination of:

1. Delivering a compelling guiding vision.
2. Strengthening or developing the necessary skills for staff.
3. Aligning resources and incentives.
4. Having a clear action plan.[1]

QUESTIONS THAT LEAD TO CHANGE

Is the need to change urgent?

Do I have support?

Do I have a vision?

Do I have a plan?

Can I communicate it?

Can I remove barriers?

Can I reinforce new behaviors?

Can I maintain the new culture?

FIGURE 3.1   Questions That Lead to Change

The first step on the path begins with "why" and "why now." This quote from Jim Rohn sums it up nicely: "Without a sense of urgency, desire loses its value."

Why and Why Now

Think back to a time when grocery stores first introduced reusable shopping bags. At the time of introduction, the grocery store offered a discount to use your own bags rather than taking the plastic or paper available at check-out. Many people started using their own bags and the discount covered the cost of purchasing that bag and then some. After a wider level of acceptance, the grocery stores stopped providing the discount. Now that several years have passed, many people are reverting to using plastic or paper unless a law requires the store to charge for a bag. In a similar manner, healthcare is using value-based payments as an incentive to encourage providers to adopt an approach that improves health outcomes and lowers cost. Regulation may occur more broadly in the future to encourage adoption of value-based care. Those that adopt early are likely to see the greatest rewards like the example of being paid to bring your own shopping bag.

Unlike the grocery store example, change to value-based care is neither as simple or quick as buying a reusable shopping bag. Those that wait to transform may find that they are adopting a value-based care approach in a time of penalties rather than incentives. While this may increase the level of urgency to adopt change, the risk of failure also increases. Working toward transforming your practice and creating a culture that supports flexibility, maximizing individual potential for both staff and patients, and focusing on generating positive health outcomes will place you ahead of your competitors. Having a plan to manage the change minimizes the risks of being an early adopter.

The reasons for change (why) and the risk of not changing (why now) will be a driving force throughout the process. The cost of healthcare is unsustainable. Something needs to change. Defining that "something" has gone through multiple iterations in both industry trends and regulatory action. Yet, the same problems continue to plague the industry. When will healthcare actually change? To be successful in transforming a practice, a sense of urgency must be present. Otherwise, the change will be classified as a nice idea but not a "must have." In any organization there will always be competing priorities for resources and people who enjoy the status quo. These two forces can reinforce a culture that avoids change.

Complacency is the death toll for change. People have many reasons for feeling that everything should stay just as it is. Or they may say "yes, but." With the "yes, but" person, there may be some acknowledgement that improvements could be made, but the person has an offsetting list of reasons why change cannot or does not need to happen. A sense of urgency can be hard to attain until either revenues or profits drop. This creates a reactive approach instead of a proactive one, where people adapt before a crisis develops.

At other times, the culture of the organization may be in a state of constantly putting out fires, which detracts from strategically deploying resources to prepare for the future. If your practice is operating in crisis mode, some actions that may break the cycle include working through the planning stages, exhibiting leadership that incorporates change management techniques, and building a culture of continuous improvement. Operating in crisis mode can look like the following:

1. Issue occurs
2. Surprise
3. Limited information
4. React to issue
5. Panic
6. Short-term thinking
7. Back to step one: issue occurs

What you notice in this cycle is lack of planning, monitoring, and assessing reliable information. These are three key elements that define an organization that is proactive rather than reactive. If you find that you are always in a reactive mode, with and plans and schedules consistently thrown off, you may need to assess the underlying causes. While a crisis often grabs attention and highly motivates people to change, operating by crisis is exhausting.

When a new initiative is discussed, feedback can be along the lines of "we are already stretched thin, how can you expect us to do more?" Rarely will you come across a person in a work environment that says they do not have enough work. Most people enjoy the comfort of feeling competent and a certain amount of routine. If the message is something that people do not want to hear, denial is a strong influencer. This is particularly true when there are no signs reinforcing the required change.

Other factors that can influence the belief that change is not needed are cultural factors such as transparency and how rewards are established. While transparency has become quite the buzz word, it is true that when employees are unaware of performance or financial results, they may not feel a sense of urgency for change. This often comes down to the principle of "what's in it for me" or WIIFM. Understanding how change or the lack of change will impact everyone is important in succeeding in true transformation.

If people are unaware of performance, or if standards of performance are set too low, there is no way for those individuals to associate negative repercussions for continuing to do business as usual. For some practices, initiating value-based care may be the first time for setting internal benchmarks or a significant expansion beyond traditional standards such as appointment availability, receivables, and claims denials. Without sharing and discussing the organization's performance compared to standards, staff have no way of determining how performance stacks up. This applies to goals for the individual, the practice, and the larger organization. Having individual goals that tie to the overarching goals of the practice and organization is a great way to encourage people to feel invested in performance and understand how individual roles and responsibilities fit in the larger picture.

Setting standards requires goals that are achievable (so that the goal is not viewed as the carrot that is dangled just out of reach). Goals should be set to encourage performance at the highest levels while not being either too easy or too hard. Disclosing information is tricky. The picture drawn should not lull people into a false sense of security; nor should it paint a picture of doom and gloom that incites fear and creates a defeatist attitude.

When open communication and feedback are not encouraged, an environment of fear is created. When a "shoot the messenger" work environment exists, people are afraid to speak up or present alternative ideas. In this type of environment, people will avoid taking risks and resist change. Or worse, they will subtly and quietly stir informal networks to ensure that failure is blamed on someone other than themselves. In these fear cultures, finger-pointing and blame are common. If there is a failure, someone needs to be the scapegoat.

The goal of answering "why" and "why now" is to raise awareness and create a sense of urgency. By reading this book, you may have taken the first step toward creating that sense of urgency. In reviewing the scope of what is required for value-based care, you are developing an understanding of the level of effort that transformation requires. When transforming a practice to participate in value-based care, depending on how your current practice operates and is structured, the process could take anywhere from six months to two years. At least one year is needed to develop baseline data, unless you were already collecting information that can be used for quality measures.

Start to create a sense of urgency by discussing the risks of the status quo and focusing on future opportunities (and related rewards that are possible with transformation).

Creating organizational goals for your practice that are tied to value-based care helps maintain focus within your practice, particularly if the goals are incorporated into each staff member's annual performance expectations, and compensation reflects the sharing of rewards.

Another way to create a sense of urgency is to talk with patients and major payers about their experiences and how your practice can better meet their needs. Keeping abreast of current literature, attending conferences, and talking to your peers will help you identify trends in the industry.

Risks & rewards: One potential risk is not being included in a payer network because of mandated requirements to participate in pay-for-performance programs and to demonstrate outcomes. On the flipside, a reward for changing your practice to participate in value-based payment programs is that you not only shape the participation requirements but also reap the early rewards. Often payers offer more significant incentives and rewards when rolling out a new program to encourage practices to be early adopters. As the program gains momentum, the rewards may decrease and/or the requirements may increase. By engaging early, your practice takes advantage of the fact that the requirements to participate are likely at the lowest point and rewards are the greatest.

Delaying the implementation of value-based care principles can leave your practice at a competitive disadvantage. Waiting for decreases in revenue and financial losses to occur as a way of driving your practice's sense of urgency is not recommended. While negative financial results quickly escalate the sense of urgency in your practice, recovering can be a difficult situation and could require unfavorable options like selling your practice. Plus, the stress and distraction of needing to address the administrative concerns takes away from your focus on transitioning to value-based care. Being able to clearly articulate why change is needed, and why it is needed now, is the first step to transforming your practice.

Laying the Groundwork

After developing the rationale for transforming your practice to embrace value-based care, the next steps are to ensure support from leadership, craft a vision, and define a project plan. Gaining support from leadership varies in level of difficulty, depending upon the size of your practice and the other factors discussed earlier such as fear of rocking the boat.

In larger organizations, leadership may be required at multiple levels. Not only must the overall organization support your efforts, but leadership support is also needed at the local practice site. In identifying a key leader, the person needs to have authority, credibility, and expertise. This person will be your catalyzer, creating acceptance from other members of the organization. This level of influence can include direct control over actions of other staff through a supervisory chain of command, or indirectly through informal relationships. Influence can also be exerted by someone that has control of financial resources and the ability to redirect staff needed to complete the transformation.

Acting as a champion for the project, the leader helps rally the organization around the common goal, promote open and honest communication, and foster a positive environment. The champion encourages people to perform at their maximum level, while balancing the fact that change is stressful and that each person reacts to the stress differently. The leader also lends credibility to the transition process. The selected champion can increase the level of awareness and gain buy-in from those affected by the changes.

A shared vision of what your practice will look and feel like when delivering value-based care is required. This vision can be crafted and directed not only by the leader but also by a core group of individuals that define and refine what the future will look like. A successful team is often comprised of the leaders within the practice. When considering who to include in the core group, evaluate the skills, expertise, and credibility that each person brings to the team and be sure to include individuals outside of leadership roles who contribute a special perspective or have needed creativity and skills. Within a small practice, the physician that owns the practice is likely the sole person within this group, or the office manager may be included as well if they work together closely. As the practice size increases, the group may consist of owners of the practice or physician representatives across multiple practice sites. How to define this group is based upon the specifics of your practice. It is essential to the success of this group that common goals are well-defined, appeal to members of the core group, and are rational.

Committing to "excellence" as an overarching goal generally works for establishing the first goal of the transformation process. The ultimate outcome of value-based care is to achieve the Triple Aim (see Chapter 1). All the goals need to be articulated in a vision that drives actions, motivates people to take those actions, and coordinates efforts around a common goal.

Your vision statement needs to be simple and understandable. This vision is communicated to multiple audiences and provides a framework for evaluating options and prioritizing actions. With a defined vision, only options and actions that align with the vision should be pursued. This helps everyone understand where your practice is going—and avoids the trap of chasing shiny objects that look like attractive options but do not move your practice closer to achieving the vision. When crafting a guiding vision, be sure that you appeal to the heart but are sensible in the approach. Your vision statement should reflect the following traits:

- Well-defined
  - clarity and focus provide guidance
- Appealing
  - desirable to stakeholders in your practice, e.g., owners, staff, and patients
- Visual
  - paints a picture of the desired future
- Viable
  - sets realistic, attainable goals
- Easy to convey
  - written in succinct, simple, easily understood language
- Flexible
  - allows for alternative points of view and paths

VISION STATEMENTS
6 Key Characteristics

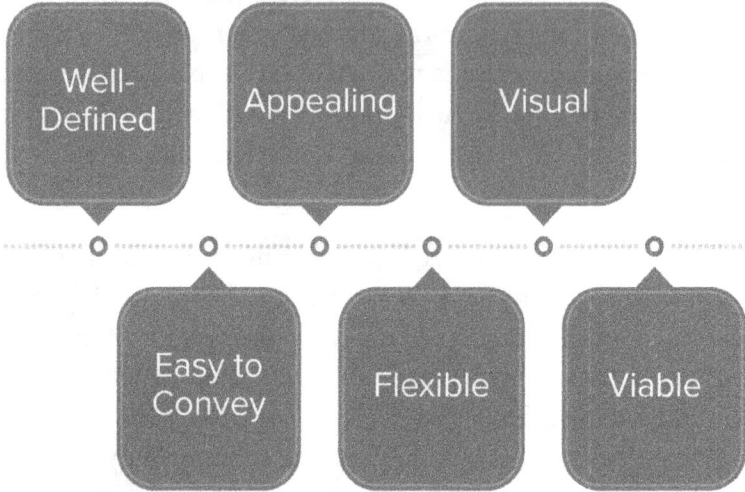

Well-Defined	Appealing	Visual

Easy to Convey	Flexible	Viable

Figure 3.2   Six Key Characteristics of Vision Statements

The process of creating your vision may be a difficult experience depending on the size of your practice or organization. The greater the number of people involved, the higher the probability for a messy process that can be rife with emotion. But your vision is important to drive forward with changing the core of how you do business. Stick with the process to create a sustaining vision and use facilitation if needed. Remember that unlike a mission statement, a vision statement should be as lengthy as needed to create a clear picture of where you are going, evoke a sense of purpose and direction, and create a call to action.

Here is an example of a potential vision statement that encompasses key elements of value-based care:

Our practice is committed to excellence and quality by delivering efficient and effective services that improve patient

health outcomes and quality of life while promoting a positive patient experience. We respect and support the concept of whole person care, encourage active patient participation, and use evidence-based principles. Our team-based delivery of care incorporates patient needs and preferences, offers flexibility, and coordinates care. We attract and retain high caliber staff that develop trusted relationships. We assess attainment of our commitment through continuous improvement and share the results of our actions with our practice, our patients, and the public.

Embedded within this vision are also the values of the organization, such as:

- Excellence
- Quality
- Respect
- Trust
- Teamwork
- Flexibility
- Continuous improvement
- Transparency

Explicitly stating values can also provide additional clarity. The end goal is to ensure that the values and vision resonate. By prioritizing aspects of the vision and values, you create a framework that allows actions to be evaluated and ranked in the same manner. This helps when difficult decisions need to be made during the process to change your organization and move toward your vision. For example, assume that there is a situation where a patient wants additional testing to be completed but the test is not recommended according to clinical guidelines and is not considered to be necessary in the judgment of the physician. To decide if the physician should order the test, you could rely upon how your practice has decided to prioritize at least three aspects of the vision. For example, using three aspects from the previously stated practice vision:

- Use of evidence-based practices (principles)—the test is not specified in clinical guidelines.
- Incorporating patient needs and preferences—the patient states desire to have test.
- Efficient use of care—the test is unnecessary and creates waste and additional costs in consuming both time and resources.

If your organization creates a hierarchy for evaluating competing demands that fall within the vision, staff have an easier time in talking with a patient about the testing and concluding what is in the best interest of everyone involved. As a word of caution, you need to follow your commitment to the vision and hierarchy in every instance. Otherwise, the vision loses credibility and people view the statement as meaningless. Alignment between words and actions is critical as you work to transform your practice's operations. If you do not, gaining cooperation and buy-in to change, and then cement that change permanently are undermined.

Planning the Project

So how does a practice get from vision to action? After the vision and values are clarified, communicated, and prioritized, you establish the roadmap of how to achieve the vision. Working through a high-level project plan with specific milestones helps to evaluate the timing and feasibility of the transformation process. Begin by comparing your strengths and areas needing improvement—which you identified in the assessment of your current operating practice—against the desired end state under value-based care as defined in Chapter 2.

Prioritize the areas needing improvement and determine what is feasible given timing and resources. The project plan defines action steps to achieve the end goals with specific due dates. The plan also identifies the lead person responsible for the task and other resources such as supporting staff and funding. A successful plan has the financial and personnel resources necessary to complete the tasks within the specified timeframe. If your practice has project planning software and the resources to maintain the plan, a more advanced plan can be used. Project planning software can identify dependencies that determine variances to plan and the impact of delays. However, a simple project plan can easily be managed in a spreadsheet program like Microsoft © Excel ©. As with the vision, the key is to keep information as simple as possible while encapsulating all the necessary components. Simplicity helps with conveying information and keeping the process manageable.

The Communication Plan

When working to establish a new way of performing and delivering care in your practice, you need to communicate regularly and consistently. Only 14% of companies have employees that understand their organization's strategy, goals, and direction.[2] As you work through the transformation process, develop a communication plan that addresses how and what you will communicate to all levels of staffing. This plan identifies how often messages will be sent, the mode of communication, who delivers the message, and the general content. With any communication, addressing key characteristics helps to prevent misinformation.

Characteristics

Given that you are communicating with people at different levels of experience and education, keeping the messaging as simple as possible is essential. Healthcare is an industry full of jargon and acronyms. Leave out the jargon or acronyms when communicating. Simple language works best. Skip big and complicated words and save showing off the range of your vocabulary for another time. Check all your communication against these characteristics:

- Concise
  - Keep it as short as possible: you are competing for attention.

ROADMAPS TO VALUE-BASED PROFITABILITY

- Conversational
  - ○ Use simple language that you speak every day.
- Colorful
  - ○ Use metaphors, analogies, and examples as appropriate.
- Clear
  - ○ Employ direct language that contains and explains all necessary information.
- Correct
  - ○ Check all information for accuracy.
- Consistent
  - ○ Deliver a core message that remains the same over time.

6 Cs OF COMMUNICATION

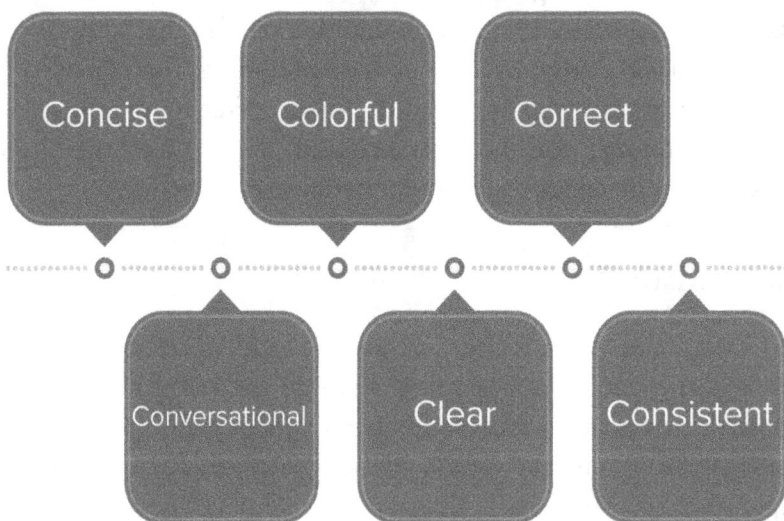

FIGURE 3.3   The Six Cs of Communication

Examining all communication against the above characteristics reduces the chances of the message being disregarded or misunderstood. When crafting your communication, consider your audience. Try to anticipate questions, reactions, or areas for potential misunderstanding. Considering these aspects helps to ensure that you addressed information adequately. By anticipating multiple types of reactions, you are also better prepared to respond to questions or may identify the need to rewrite the message to increase the likelihood of a positive reception.

Modes of Communication

How you communicate is as important as *what* you communicate. You need to use more than one way of communicating. Your options include formal and informal communication, and a mix of styles is effective.

Email is a common way for communicating information. With the volume of information that is floating around, people are suffering from information overload. An average employee will spend 28% of the work week (13 hours) reading and responding to e-mail, according the McKinsey Global Institute.[3] Emails are often subject to misinterpretation in content and tone. To increase the likelihood that your message is received, do not use email as your only form of communication.

After tailoring your message to your audience(s), some ways of communicating are:

- Meetings
  - ideally face-to-face or video conference
- Bulletin board
  - post important information in a central location
- Newsletter
  - great for regularly delivering highlights of the message
- Hold a Retreat
  - a face-to-face meeting held away from the workplace
  - useful for brainstorming, connecting people, and communicating critical or complicated information

- Social media and other technology
  - ○ Twitter, YouTube and texting are popular and convenient
- E-mail
  - ○ written communication can be effective, particularly as a follow-up after verbal communication

When developing your communication plan, be sure to consider the delivery of information. The preferred method for communicating significant news, like transforming the way your practice functions, is through a face-to-face meeting. Based on statistics from *Forbes*, direct communication is primarily filtered by the audience based on facial expressions and body language (55%), and tone (37%), with only 8% on the words.[4] With non-verbal communication affecting more than half the message, being prepared for delivering the message is essential. Practice the delivery of what you are communicating before presenting verbal information. Repetition of information creates confidence, and confidence evokes positive reactions.

Hearing information about change presents both an intellectual and emotional challenge. Everyone processes new information differently. Creating main points and themes are useful in ensuring that communication stays consistent and the content is clear. The person delivering the message also impacts how information is received and processed. For large scale issues, the CEO or top leader of your practice is likely to have better reception than delegating the message to someone else. A direct supervisor, however, is a better choice for delivering information about changes related to a person's specific role.

Content

As you tackle communicating about your practice's future operations, and what change is needed today to achieve that vision, you should consider what information to share. Depending on your audience, the concept of practice transformation to value-based care may be foreign. You may need to explain the broader context of what is occurring in the healthcare industry to raise awareness of the need for transforming how you deliver care.

Not everyone in your practice is aware of the competing demands and pressures to change the core of how healthcare is delivered. Communicating information about the broader context of the changes in healthcare helps to explain why change is necessary. You can then follow this information with the message outlining changes to how your practice delivers care. This messaging should be tied to the mission of the organization. The vision of what your practice's future looks like is a key component in any communication plan. The vision creates the guiding goals for transformation. Ensuring that everyone understands the vision is essential.

The next part of the communication plan is to provide an overview of the outcomes to be achieved. Define how you will know whether the practice transformation is successful. Timelines and specific actions are important to communicate as well. However, your message should focus more on the "why" rather than solely on the "what." You will need to address what is changing and how that will happen.

People want to understand not only the basic information, but they also filter everything based on the WIIFM principle. It is important that you tailor your communication to address these concerns for your audience. Other tailoring includes ensuring the appropriate reading level, language, and level of detail in information. As part of your planning process, the types of questions you expect to receive should be considered, and developing answers is a proactive approach to anticipating and addressing reactions.

After sharing information, be sure to slow down and listen to comments, questions, or concerns. Ensure that you truly listen to what people are saying and resist jumping to respond too quickly. Otherwise you may miss what is being said. Also, the quick response is not always the best response. At times you may want to take back the information and feedback and consider all the options before responding. However, it is important that follow-up occurs, and that a response is made to close the communication loop, reaching all participants in the original conversation.

Providing the option for people to share additional comments, questions, or concerns after hearing information for the first time is also recommended. Some individuals may not be comfortable speaking immediately, others may need time after to process what has been communicated. Ensuring there are many ways for your audience to share and question information is important allows full participation, even if it isn't in real time.

After making sure everyone understands the "why" and the "why now," the content of your communication will focus on how the practice needs to transform. Keep staff informed about what changes are going to happen and how these changes will impact each of them. Regular updates reinforce your messaging and support the change process. As you shift your practice operations, success stories should be shared along the way. Especially in times of change, you cannot communicate enough. If you think you have communicated enough, say it again.

Eliminate Obstacles

As people listen to your message and process how they will be affected by the change, fear and uncertainly may elicit negative reactions. Providing the necessary training and resources to build skills eases some of those concerns. During times of change, ensuring people feel necessary and useful is empowering. As you work to transform your practice, you need to eliminate obstacles that prevent growth and change. Some of these obstacles could be based on the structure of your practice and overall organization.

Many businesses face difficulties in coordinating employees. Silos develop with people acting in their own best interest, sometimes to protect their turf. This behavior can be intentional, but more often it is found when the workplace does not support collaboration or encourage a 360° view. Take a broad view of how actions impact others up and down the chain of command as well as horizontally. Each person should be encouraged to consider how actions affect others, not only including internal staff, but also patients and vendors. Other challenges that need to be addressed are the levels of authority, financing, and the sense of personal loss that may be experienced during times of change.

Leadership has a deep impact on the success of the transformation through actions. The individual actions of leaders must be consistent with what has been conveyed about the future. Staff need encouragement. Leadership and direct supervisors should act as role-models to deliver on the vision of value-based care. As the level of stress increases within the practice, everyone should be aware of instances where decisions are undermined, or people are playing backseat driver and second-guessing decisions. Individuals resisting change may use these two tactics to derail transformation efforts. Work to increase your level of awareness, be alert for these types of behavior, and intercede as necessary.

Part of the operational transformation is to become more patient-focused. Although many practices would say that they are already patient-focused, you may realize as you read through this book that placing the patient at the center of all decisions is harder than expected, and not truly what you are delivering today. Training must focus on more than just good customer service—although that is a critical underlying element. You also need to provide training so that people are prepared for situations that are different from how work is handled today. This may involve breaking old practice patterns and habits to develop a new perspective and appreciation for how care must be delivered under a value-based approach.

Staff should be encouraged to think creatively and focus on solutions rather than barriers. To do this, they must be able to act, even if the actions do not follow traditional hierarchy and practices. This is particularly true with team-based care, which will be covered in more detail in Chapter 8.

The practice's training should reinforce and support the content of the communication plan. It may be helpful to provide additional training on increasing personal awareness and emotional intelligence. At a managerial level, focus on team building, coaching or mentoring, and employee empowerment. For employees, training skills should focus on customer service and functioning as a team member.

With the shift to value-based care, new technical skills may also be necessary. When looking at outcomes and incorporating quality improvement into your practice, the use of data to inform decisions and provide feedback about the success of change becomes part of daily, routine operations. Some barriers to communicating the data used to support decisions include staff who are intimidated by numbers or who lack the analytical skills required. Providing training about outcomes, the types of data to be presented, and what will be done with the information can create a certain level of comfort with basic information.

Ensuring consistency in human resource functions like performance evaluations, compensation, promotion, recruitment, and hiring is another way to eliminate obstacles to change. Incentives should align with annual performance evaluations where compensation, promotion, and recognition are given to those individuals that support and encourage adoption of change. When individuals are rewarded or recognized but do not act in a manner consistent with the vision and principles of value-based care, other members of staff will not believe in the vision as they see actions contradicting the words. Remember – actions speak louder than words.

Reinforcing the Changes

An effective way to encourage people to stay motivated during a time of change is to plan and achieve short-term wins. Celebrating successes builds credibility and momentum. After the initial enthusiasm for creating a new way to deliver care, people will find juggling daily responsibilities while shifting how the practice operates challenging. Sustaining the mental energy and dedication to reach the end goal requires attention and support. At times there will be a lull in progress.

As with any process that hits a plateau then scales, transforming your practice will need phased strategies. Plan for short-term wins along the way to keep focus on the transition and keep enthusiasm up. Everyone involved in the transformation process needs to see the win, determine that the results are real, and associate the positive activity with the transition efforts. This helps combat the cynics and people resisting change.

Planning for early successes is often overlooked when implementing significant changes. The workload may feel overwhelming, but do not let that prevent you from identifying how to deliver early wins. If the vision guiding the transformation is not clear, determining what can be accomplished and celebrated may be difficult to determine. Finding ways to achieve positive outcomes tends to be easier in smaller organizations and with shorter projects. The longer the project, the more important planning successes throughout the project becomes. Momentum is easy to build but hard to sustain. That is why it is important to build success during all phases of the project and not just during the early stages.

Just as you had to develop the support for transforming how you operate, you need to maintain that support. This requires balancing short-term needs and goals with the long-term results. The sense of urgency needed for the change process can never dwindle while the transformation is progressing. Otherwise people will think that what has been accomplished so far is enough and that no further work needs to be completed. You may also encounter people that sit back waiting to see which way the wind blows before determining if supporting the project is worth the effort or in their best interest.

Resistance to change never fully disappears. If the project fumbles or goes slightly off-track, the quiet resisters can work to undermine progress and the need for additional change. In some cases, the people that resisted changing may even work to celebrate successes, then quietly convey the message that the hard work is over and that taking a break from change and having a period of calm will not affect the overall outcome. However, if this message succeeds in changing the overall attitude, the progress will be put aside. When the urgency to continue transitioning dissipates, regaining momentum and recovering from the stalled period is very difficult.

Training and skill development increase the ability of team members to function effectively. To change the workflows and processes, the team members need to understand the reasons for change, how daily work is affected, and to find the personal motivation to accept and support the change. This leads back to the need for training. The interdependency of training and workflows cannot be over-emphasized. When working through the planning and actual transition, instances will occur where one change leads to another which could lead to yet another change. When this occurs, remember to step back, consider the bigger picture, and evaluate your priorities.

> **Setbacks often happen because of interdependencies.** In many cases, your initial assessment of the amount of change to existing operations will be underestimated. When you find that one change requires multiple changes to other parts of the practice or organization, evaluate whether all parts of the process are necessary. If no value is generated by the process, eliminate unnecessary steps or actions. Applying concepts of continuous quality improvement, as discussed in Chapter 12, to internal operations and functions is an added benefit of the change process.

Once celebrating wins is in place and momentum is building based on these successes, you may find that more change is occurring than you anticipated. This is a milestone that lets you know support and acceptance have been gained from much of the staff impacted by the transformation effort. As people become more engaged in transforming how your organization operates, continuing evolution and change is easier. In the ideal situation, the concept of continuous improvement has been fostered and staff are actively looking for ways to improve. The role of leadership becomes more about ensuring the urgency felt is vision-based, and less about driving the change. Individuals at all levels of the organization intentionally change and refine processes. Components of the plan are delegated downward, and frontline mid-level staff are actively leading change efforts. In a truly successful transformation, the new way of delivering care becomes a routine part of daily work life.

Keeping the New Culture

Within every organization, unwritten rules exist that define the general environment within the office and expected behavior. These shared values and behaviors represent the culture. Culture tends to survive change despite people coming and going. Generally, everyone knows what culture feels like even if defining what makes the culture is difficult. The culture can vary at different levels or locations. To be successful in transforming the delivery of care, the culture must be:

- Consistent and patient-focused
- Supportive of the team concept
- Data-oriented to improve care and health outcomes
- Acclimated toward continuous improvement

Changing culture involves fighting against an attitude of "this is the way we have always done things." Managing the culture requires encouraging the desired behaviors and attitudes, while eliminating negative influences. Turning a blind eye to problems undermines the transformation process. The office will stagnate, and the environment will not shift as you planned. During a successful change process, the culture converts to support the vision. Because these changes are relatively new, continuing to encourage the change is much like nurturing a plant. When growing a plant from a seed, the seedling first sprouts in a small amount of soil with fragile, thin roots. As the seedling grows larger, the plant must be transplanted to a larger pot to allow deeper roots, or it will choke on its own growth. The plan also needs water and sun to grow. If you do not pay attention to all the basic needs of the plant, it will die. Changing culture is the same as growing a full-sized plant from a seed.

61

Individuals involved in the change need to part ways with old habits and create new habits. To encourage the change in culture you need to:

- Demonstrate results that show improvement occurs because of the new model of care.
- Acknowledge what has been done well in the past but show how it will no longer be successful in the future.
- Prepare for departures by individuals who do not accept the new culture; consider offering incentives for voluntary departure for anyone not on board with the new vision.
- Hire new staff who align with the new culture.
- Ensure there is recognition that promotes the values of the new culture.

Continuous Assessment

As with any process, you need to evaluate whether the change was successful. Throughout the transformation process, regularly check how the process is received—and if the expected outcomes were realized. A vision of the future is something that never is fully achieved. When you get close to your original vision, you will likely find that the vision can be improved based on more current information. Continuous improvement requires that you evaluate actions to determine the *actual* results against *desired* results, tweaking the program as necessary. The basics of continuous improvement are defined in further detail in Chapter 12.

Finding the Practice's Competitive Advantage

Tackling the process of transforming the underlying core of how you do business is no small feat, but it is necessary to remain competitive. Sitting back and waiting to see which way the wind blows may seem easier than forcing change. It may feel safer to let others test the waters and see if value-based care is successful and stands the test of time—but playing the wait-and-see game could be catastrophic.

To make a lasting transformation, your practice must adopt new ways of delivering care with new attitudes and behaviors which are reinforced, recognized, and rewarded. Building the capacity for change into your daily strategies will allow the practice to remain viable and competitive. As Benjamin Franklin once said, "When you're finished changing, you're finished."

CHAPTER 4

What Do Your Patients Have in Common?

Many providers find the vast amount of clicking required to document the patient visit frustrating. Structuring your practice to make the annoyance of collecting data result in information that improves patient lives can increase acceptance of documentation requirements. This is not to discourage the idea of creating better templates and minimizing clicking, but rather to seek usefulness in the data. The EHR and practice management system collect a wealth of data, but the data is useless unless you can gain insights from it. Value is found in the data collected through extracting and analyzing the results in a meaningful way (that allows for better management of your patients).

Having data that does not result in action is just like a book sitting on a shelf collecting dust—the value comes from what information you take from the book and implement in your practice. The same is true for data. The use of data to better inform care is at the core of population health. Managing population health starts with looking at the common characteristics of your patients. Developing a strong understanding of your patients is the first step to impacting overall care in terms of both cost and quality—two-thirds of the goals of the Triple Aim. Every practice should be moving toward population health management as part of transformation efforts.

Population Health

Population health is defined as the health outcomes of a group individuals, including the distribution of such outcomes within the group.[1] Health outcomes are defined as more than the absence of disease. Multiple influences impact population health,[2] including:

- Access to care
- Understanding of health
- Prevention and management of chronic conditions
- Socioeconomic factors
  - income
  - availability of food
  - other social determinants of health.[3]

Population health management involves a continuous cycle of assessing performance data, setting goals, identifying appropriate interventions, engaging patients, coordinating and improving care delivery, and determining if the desired outcome or goal of interventions was achieved before starting over again. Embedding this concept within your practice is the end goal. The steps are:

1. Set goals
2. Identify interventions
3. Engage patient
4. Coordinate care
5. Measure and assess performance
6. Using information from step five, return to step one

The goal of population health management is to improve the overall health of the patients served in such a way that it influences the surrounding community. With a full ripple effect, health improvement spreads beyond the local community to across a broad range of populations, including a state, a whole nation, or potentially the world.

The starting point of population health is understanding the characteristics of the patients you serve. By analyzing various data points, you will develop an understanding of not only the medical conditions being experienced by your patients but also what issues and concerns are present that could be impeding the patients from maintaining or improving their health. By understanding a broad picture of your patient panel, you can start to assess how your practice can be transformed to meet the overall needs of your patients. Start by looking at what your patients have in common. Understanding the bigger picture can help direct resources in structuring staffing, knowing what educational information to have available, and which clinical guidelines to implement. By gearing your practice to address common concerns and medical conditions, your providers and clinical team will have a solid foundation for tailoring care to individual patient needs.

Getting to Know Your Patient Population

To prepare for accepting value-based payment models, you must understand who you serve. When you consider what your patient panel looks like, what characteristics first come to mind? Maybe the first thoughts are based on demographics, like age and race, or possibly certain diagnoses or conditions that are most commonly treated in the practice. How the patient panel is described may vary for each person within the practice and across practice sites. Understanding a broad picture of who you serve across your practice and organization allows for breaking down the patient population, and related data, into subsets.

Comparisons between providers and practice sites can lead to identifying variations in practice patterns. The variations in practice patterns can be evaluated to learn what works best on a wide level. This type of analysis is not intended to create a cookie cutter approach to how care is delivered, but rather to allow for a deeper understanding of what is a normal approach to care, which can then be applied to individuals and tailored when deviations are needed. Before addressing what data is available, understanding some basics about the data stored in the information systems is helpful.

Data Basics

Each performance management and EHR system is configured based upon preferences of the organization and, potentially, individual users. Data collected on the screens viewed by the end user is stored in some form of data tables. Describing how data is stored and can be accessed is beyond the scope of this book, aside from noting that data is generally accessible for reporting with the right knowledge and tools. One resource for digging deeper into reporting and having the right tools is Nate Moore's *Even Better Data, Better Decisions*. However, it can be useful to understand how data is stored within the system to gain a firmer grasp of the possibilities. Understanding the difference between structured and unstructured data can clarify the functionality of the system and the importance of mandatory fields.

Structured data is organized, and unstructured data is not. According to HIMSS, structured data is defined as "data organized into specific fields as part of a schema, with each field having a defined purpose. Data can be structured within each field(s) through data validation—by enforcing use of a standardized data format or allowing only a specific range of values entered in a field." In simple terms, structured data represents information that can be classified as yes/no (think of a checkbox as being converted to yes if marked and no if not checked), date, or alphanumeric. Structured data allows for only the defined data to be entered into a field through either validation rules (i.e., not allowing a date to be entered if numbers are not used and the specific format is not followed) or the use of drop-down boxes to control potential answers.

Unstructured data is not easily organized in pre-defined structures and is more challenging to us for reporting. Within the EHR, a text box where you can write a note is an example of unstructured data. To use unstructured data, the logic of the program to generate a report would need to interpret what is written in the note. While this can be done, the reliability of the data is limited.

To illustrate the difference in how structured and unstructured data are used in creating a report, imagine you are running a report assessing whether a copay was collected. If the copay information was written in a text box, you might be able to look for the word "copay," in the hopes that everyone enters the word "copay" before adding the dollar amount. Depending on how the logic is created for that word, you may find information about copays, but creating a calculable report with dollar amounts would be difficult. The data from an unstructured field cannot be aggregated or tabulated, resulting in information that is hard to manipulate. However, if the copay is entered directly into a field that is labeled "copay" and requires entry as a number or dollar amount, a report can be created based on this structured data. The report can assess any formula based on the copay such as sum or average.

Where practices may encounter difficulties is when there are fields with similar descriptions and the source of the data is unclear. It can be common for IT or reporting staff to develop the report without understanding where data is captured by the end-user. This can lead to frustration between both parties, as the point of reference for looking at the data is different. Those developing the reports are looking at the data tables where information is stored, while the end-user will only know where the data appears on a specific screen. If the two are disconnected, you may run a report using a specific data field from a data table, but the data is not populated correctly. This can occur when there is more than one field for a data element, as a result of more than one screen having a place for the end-user to enter the data and unclear direction about which field to use, These sorts of discrepancies are often found when new reports are generated.

In an ideal situation, there should be only one location to record a discrete data point. Unfortunately, that is not always the case. For example, in the early stages of meaningful use data reporting, practices would find that the data did not match what the providers intuitively knew from entering data during office visits. To identify why the data was showing low results, the logic of the report had to be examined. The report was pulling from one field that had an area for recording the blood pressure (BP) reading. However, in practice, the BP reading was being recorded on a different screen, which was captured in a different data field.

To get the most accurate results, either everyone needed clear directions as to where the BP reading must be recorded so that data was collected and reported accurately, or, the less desirable alternative, the report needed to be modified to look in the two different locations. The risk with the report looking in two locations is that data could be double counted or somehow incorrectly represented. These types of issues should be kept in mind as you review what data is captured and in which screens. This will be valuable information to convey when creating reports to characterize your patient population and other reports needed for gaining deeper insights about who you serve.

Starting with the Easy Stuff

Within the data you capture to bill for services is a host of information that you can use to understand the basic characteristics of your patient population. At a minimum, to bill for a service, you need to verify insurance coverage if applicable, the billable procedure code, the diagnosis, and the date of service. Payers use this information to generate sophisticated analytics about members served. This same data is readily available within your practice—along with additional data not necessarily available to payers. Understanding how to use this information is important in practicing value-based care.

As part of enrolling a new patient into a practice—or updating existing records—the practice gathers demographics like age, gender, insurance, and contact information. With the introduction of meaningful use, many practices expanded the data collection to gather even more information. Additionally, within each patient record is current data like vitals and lab results, information that may not be accessible to the payer. The lab tests and vitals can be leading indicators for individuals at risk of developing a chronic condition or experiencing progression or regression of an existing condition. Using this data to identify individuals that need more proactive management for prevention is a significant way to avoid future costs. Disrupting the rate of healthcare spending is essential for population health management, which is tied to more advanced forms of value-based payments like gain and risk sharing arrangements.

Demographic Data

Essential facts are contained within demographic data. By its definition, demographic data includes statistical data that describes some socioeconomic characteristics of a given population. Previously, within the medical community, the demographic data collected often did not include information about income level and education, which are examples of two socioeconomic factors. With the emphasis on addressing how social determinants of health affect overall health and outcomes, collecting and using this data helps to refine your understanding of your patients. The importance of collecting information about socioeconomic factors is gaining traction. Understanding what the factors are and how they impact the needs of your patients is discussed in greater detail in Chapter 5. Expanding the collection of basic information at patient registration, with regular verification and updates, can assist your practice to have deeper knowledge of your patients and better anticipate and meet their needs.

With the advent of EHRs, capturing of basic demographic information has become centralized. Many providers took advantage of incentives to implement EHRs after CMS introduced the Electronic Health Records Incentive Program in 2011. This program was rolled out in three stages over several years and was designed to demonstrate meaningful use of certified EHR technology.

In return for submitting measures and meeting certain thresholds, providers were paid an incentive. Although this incentive has stopped, many practices are continuing to capture much of the data that had been required to qualify for the incentive. Often referred to as meaningful use or MU measures, the demographic data to be captured included:

- Date of birth
  - patient birth date, collected as MM/DD/YYYY
- Sex or gender
  - as of 2019, defined as male or female
- Race
  - defined by categories published by the Office of Management and Budget (OMB)
- Ethnicity
  - defined by categories published by the OMB[4]
- Preferred language
  - primary language patient uses to communicate

Additionally, as part of general data collection during patient registration, practices collect information regarding the patient's home address, telephone number, and e-mail address. When collecting the data, the information system often has drop-down boxes to select fields that are limited to certain answers—such as race or ethnicity. Data fields may require that certain criteria be met, such as whether the year of birth is collected as a 2-digit (YY) or 4-digit (YYYY) year. Rules within the EHR often prevent users from entering the wrong number of characters (i.e., entering 18 instead of 2018 for year). This is a data validation technique which helps prevent invalid data from being entered. Another example of data validation is to prevent the use of a letter as a character, allowing only numeric values instead. An example of when this rule would be used is in the entry of the ZIP Code within the United States.

For reporting and data analysis, using structured data fields that have specific data validation requirements provides the most flexibility. This basic demographic data allows for segmenting the patient population and is particularly useful when assessing for disparities in care.

Diagnosis and Procedure Codes

In capturing information about services delivered, at least one diagnosis is identified, as well as at least one procedure code. These two core elements, the diagnosis code and the procedure code, capture information about each patient. With the introduction of ICD-10, the diagnosis code can have a level of granular specificity not previously captured. The diagnosis code can be used as a key data element to examine how many patients have a certain diagnosis—or aggregate by diagnostic group. By identifying multiple diagnosis codes within a single visit, multiple issues can be documented.

Further analysis based on the procedure code billed and the frequency of visits provides additional visibility on the complexity of the patient's needs. Insurance companies use this same type of data to analyze provider performance, and routinely review diagnoses and procedure codes submitted on claims or encounters. Being able to think like a payer, including understanding who you serve and what your trends in utilization and cost are, will help maximize a practice's profit. When analyzed, this information can provide insight on how to impact utilization, cost, and health outcomes. Understanding and implementing these controls are important for succeeding in negotiating additional payments or higher reimbursement under value-based payment methodologies.

Payers go through a similar analytical approach when bidding on contracts like Medicaid and large employer groups. Assessing the prior utilization cost creates the baseline. The payer then determines where the cost curve can be bent and quality improved. While your practice does not need to go through a full actuarial underwriting analysis, adopting this approach on the smaller, more manageable scale can help identify essential elements of your practice and guide where to change the office processes, and how care is managed.

Extracting the data from your billing system is a great starting place for identifying the characteristics of your patients. If you can further combine the billing data with clinical data such as blood pressure readings, A1c levels, or other relevant tests for a specific diagnosis, you start to create a richer picture of your patient population. This involves taking information you may currently have set up as a registry or report and taking it one step further. For example, you may already have a report that shows patients that have poor control of blood sugar with an A1c level greater than 9. If you were able to understand more about the patients that have these higher levels, by analyzing additional data points, you may see if there are patterns that suggest a need for a new approach to engaging patients or understanding additional risks.

Information that you should have readily available within any existing systems includes:

- Demographics
- Type of insurance
- How often patients are seen
- Diagnosis
- Types of visits (procedure code)
- Frequency of reschedules or no-show

Additionally, if you can capture information about emergency department visits and inpatient admissions, you can further identify patterns that may indicate the need for a different approach to engaging the patient, or potentially a need to recommend additional supports.

General Health Outcomes and Factors

Another source for gathering information about what your patient may be experiencing is to look at general health outcomes and health factors. By knowing generalities of the local community, you may find that certain educational information or referral community supports are needed, even if the patient does not discuss these needs. General characteristics for every county in the USA can be found at the website http://www.countyhealthrankings.org. This data is collected from multiple sources, including the Centers for Disease Control and Prevention (CDC). Each county within a state is ranked for health outcomes based on two measures: how long people live and how healthy people feel while alive.

For the ranking by health factors, the measures include health behaviors, clinical care, social and economic, and physical environment factors. Detailed information for each county can be found at the website, providing insight into the whole community. This also provides a potential benchmark for comparing statistics and characteristics of your patient population. For example, if you are tracking the number of adult patients with a BMI over 30 and classified as obese, you can compare the percentage of patients in your practice to the overall number within your county. If it is significantly different, then you may have an underlying issue within your practice. By focusing on weight control, you may have a positive impact on the patient and the surrounding community as desired by the end goal of population health. In a brief produced by the Kaiser Family Foundation, it was noted that "social factors, including education, racial segregation, social supports and poverty accounted for over a third of total deaths in the United States in a year."[5]

Finding Out What You Know

Start using your data to review the characteristics of who you serve to better structure your practice to meet their needs. When starting to evaluate the characteristics of your patient population, you need to know what information is available, where it is stored in the system, and how to retrieve the relevant data. Finally, the data must be interpreted. Gathering information about what data is collected in your EHR and practice management systems is a good starting point. This information combined with data about socioeconomic factors (Chapter 5) can provide a deeper understanding of your patient population as your practice moves toward managing population health as described in Chapter 6.

CHAPTER 5

Understanding the Whole Picture
of Patient Health

One source of poor outcomes is the fragmentation of healthcare. With multiple participants in healthcare, patient treatment by any one doctor has become very limited. Combined with payment based on the delivery of services, regardless of outcomes, providers are pressured and forced to assess and treat patients in a short period of time.

To increase overall revenue, the focus has been on the number of patients seen in a day or total volume of visits or procedures. To gather a comprehensive perspective, a provider should be asking questions, assessing answers, and addressing factors that influence overall health. These factors include social determinants of health, unhealthy behaviors, behavioral health, and cultural competency. These factors are not necessarily considered when addressing an acute illness or chronic condition, but greatly impact patient success in maintaining a healthy lifestyle. This approach can pay off. A Humana report based on 2017 data described medical costs as being 15.6% lower for patients treated by physicians in value-based agreements than comparable FFS practices.[1]

Incorporating a review of these factors into your benchmarking and data analysis can help your practice identify barriers to care and provide insight about resources needed by your patients. Resource opportunities include:

- Provide educational materials.
- Connect patients to services and supports outside the practice.
- Develop relationships with other providers or programs.
- Expand options or services delivered by your practice in a manner that a patient can understand in terms of education and culture.

Social Determinants of Health

Social determinants of health are the social and economic factors that influence health status. In certain areas of the healthcare, social determinants of health have long been recognized as impacting health and health outcomes. But within other segments of healthcare, the identification of a social determinant may be a new concept. To those involved in programs such as Medicaid, the social determinants are often identified as barriers to care. These factors include living and working conditions, as opposed to individual risk factors such as unhealthy behaviors or genetics. Disparities in health outcomes can be related to social, economic, and physical environmental factors. According to research, these socioeconomic and physical factors account for 50% of the health components influencing quality of life and life expectancy. Clinical care only accounts for 20%, while health behaviors account for 40%.

The U.S. Federal Government created an initiative that includes population health objectives in ten-year increments. The current program is known as Healthy People 2020 (www.healthypeople.gov). Defining national health improvements and priorities, with measurable objectives and goals, Healthy People 2020 has four overarching goals:

- Attain high-quality, longer lives free of preventable disease, disability, injury, and premature death.
- Achieve health equity, eliminate disparities, and improve the health of all groups.

COMPOSITION OF HEALTH

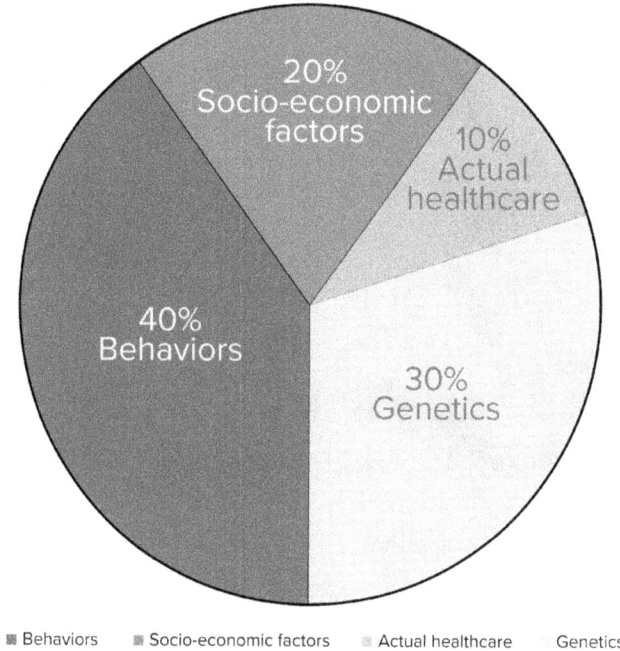

FIGURE 5.1   Composition of Health

- Create social and physical environments that promote good health for all.
- Promote quality of life, healthy development, and healthy behaviors across all life stages.

The objectives cover a wide variety of topics, including areas like social determinants, access to healthcare, heart disease and stroke, substance abuse, tobacco use, physical activity, and diabetes. Healthy People 2020 includes over 1,200 objectives in 42 different topic areas. Within these topic areas, leading health indicators (LHIs) are high priority items that have been identified as early predictors of health outcomes. Within Healthy People 2020, the following LHI were identified:

- Access to health services
- Clinical preventive services

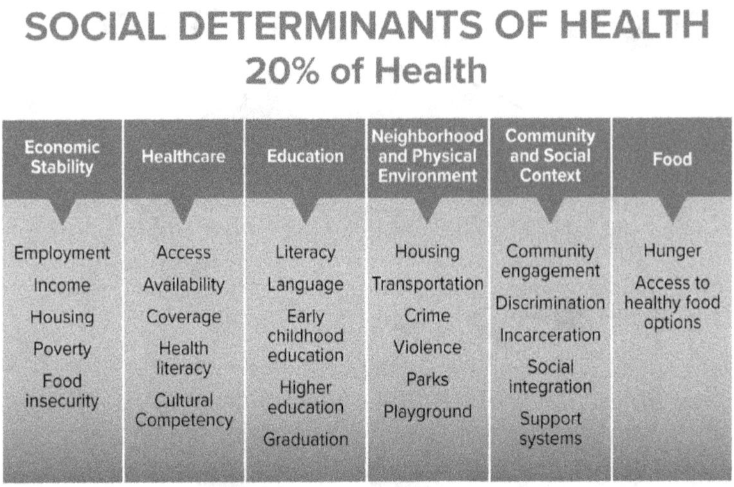

SOCIAL DETERMINANTS OF HEALTH
20% of Health

Economic Stability	Healthcare	Education	Neighborhood and Physical Environment	Community and Social Context	Food
Employment	Access	Literacy	Housing	Community engagement	Hunger
Income	Availability	Language	Transportation	Discrimination	Access to healthy food options
Housing	Coverage	Early childhood education	Crime	Incarceration	
Poverty	Health literacy		Violence	Social integration	
Food insecurity	Cultural Competency	Higher education	Parks	Support systems	
		Graduation	Playground		

FIGURE 5.2   Social Determinants of Health

- Environmental quality
- Injury and violence
- Maternal, infant, and, child health
- Nutrition, physical activity, and obesity
- Oral health
- Reproductive and sexual health
- Social determinants
- Substance abuse
- Tobacco use

Traditionally, social determinants of health have been addressed primarily in the public health sector with a heavy focus by community health centers, FQHCs, and other providers participating in public programs like Medicaid. However, understanding the impact of social determinants on health will highlight the issues and barriers patients experience that negatively affect their ability to manage their health. Health disparities arise when there are differences in the measures and outcomes between groups of people within a given population. These differences can be evaluated based on characteristics like race, ethnicity, level of income, education, and employment to name a few. Some of these characteristics may be influenced by where people live, work, and play. These are social determinants and are often the source of health disparities.

SOCIAL DETERMINANTS OF HEALTH

Sources of Health Disparities

FIGURE 5.3   Social Determinants of Health

Resources for incorporating a review of social determinants are available. Two examples of programs and initiatives are the State Innovation Models (SIM) initiative and the Protocol for Responding to and Assessing Patients' Assets, Risks and Experiences (PRAPARE).

Through the SIM initiative, CMS offers competitive bid grants. Within the second round of SIM grants, most of the eleven awardees are addressing social determinants of health with a focus on creating stronger care linkages particularly around primary care, specialty care, behavioral healthcare, public health, and community-based organizations/social supports.[2] As part of the grant, a statewide plan to improve population health was requested with, at a minimum, the three core areas of tobacco use, diabetes and obesity being addressed.

In some states, community health centers are implementing PRAPARE as a tool.[3] This tool is designed not only to collect information about social determinants of health, but also to respond to identified needs. While not every need can be addressed by your practice, with the information about where there are gaps, your practice can identify if additional services are needed that could potentially be delivered internally or decide to meet the need by developing relationships with existing providers of services. This could include relationships with more than just the medical community.

While a practice may not have the resources to address a specific need, developing an understanding and awareness of what social determinants are and how they affect the ability to manage care creates a foundation of knowledge. You may also find that changing your practice to support addressing these barriers is possible. Once your practice enters into value-based arrangements, understanding the impact social determinants of health have on patients will allow the practice to build the right approaches to improve its patients' health and meet the practice's value-based contract obligations.

A simple first step is to gather information about resources available to your patients outside of your practice that help provide education or assistance in addressing needs. An example could be how to apply for assistance with paying for utilities. Understanding the resources and supports available through the community, health plan, or local government may be enough to connect your patients to additional supports and services that are needed. When looking at the characteristics of your patient population and the local area—as noted in the general health outcomes and factors section in Chapter 4—

certain assumptions can be made about the needs of your patients and confirmed directly with patients during face to face contacts.

Unhealthy Behaviors Impacted by Social Determinants of Health

Many practices are already asking about certain behaviors that can be classified as unhealthy and increase the risk of poor health outcomes. This is the first step for a practice—to assess risk factors during the wellness visit. Living a healthy lifestyle that has a balanced approach to eating and drinking, regular exercise, and avoidance of smoking and misuse of substances is a general goal for all people. Encouraging these behaviors can be difficult depending upon the environment in which patients live.

Reasons for why people can have difficulties in engaging in healthy behaviors can range from lack of resources, such as grocery stores and fresh foods, to lack of support from the people in their lives that will encourage good choices. In low income areas, there are often a wide range of fast food options that are less expensive and more readily available than fresh vegetables and fruits. Combine that with lack of education about appropriate quantity and quality of food and how to prepare meals at home, and you have a recipe for a patient who will struggle with long-term outcomes. Addressing social determinants can be an uphill battle. First, they must be identified, and the starting point is to ask questions.

For example, start your practice's gathering of information with just five questions about availability and access to food and a safe place to exercise. Review the answers that are provided to determine which identify issues that need to be addressed. As noted, the list of social determinants covers a wide spectrum of issues. Identifying patient needs can provide insight as to why outcomes are not at desired levels. You can expand the questions to take a deeper dive into specific issues that are relevant to your patients.

Ideally, answers to key questions are embedded in each patient's medical record. Some EHR vendors are incorporating a wider range of questions that can be asked during the visit. Also, make questionnaires available that could be answered at the time of patient check-in, or even in advance of arriving at the office. The ideal situation is that the questionnaire be entered into the patient record as structured data and not a scanned document. As noted previously, structured data allows for reporting and inclusion in analysis of factors that can be addressed to improve patient health outcomes, which is required to succeed in value-based payment programs.

While screening and addressing behavioral health may identify certain behaviors, a practice should also identify and discuss unhealthy or risky behaviors that are not related to mental health or substance use. Pediatric practices often address these behaviors, particularly with adolescents and teenagers. During early childhood, a pediatric practice addresses safe behaviors, like childproofing and use of car seats with the parent or caregiver. As the patient matures, the conversation transitions to topics discussed directly with the adolescent or teen-aged patient. Often a parent/guardian is asked to leave the exam room so that the sensitive topics like sexual behavior can be addressed.

In the adult community, much of the unhealthy behaviors are focused around exercise and nutrition. For nutrition, the focus tends to be on eating habits and can probe into whether a balanced diet of healthy fats, lean protein, fruits, vegetables, and whole grains are being consumed. Additional focus can be on appropriate consumption of water, caffeine, salt, and sugar. While these types of questions may be asked more of individuals with chronic conditions like high blood pressure or diabetes, asking a patient about nutrition can identify eating patterns that should be changed proactively to prevent future illness.

Use of tobacco and alcohol are generally addressed as part of addictions and mental health. However, the inter-relatedness of the topics is easy to see, as smoking is both an unhealthy behavior and an addiction. Oftentimes, making a clear distinction is not necessary, but assessing for unhealthy or risky behaviors in addition to substance use is of value. Other ideas for unhealthy behaviors could be to ask about seatbelt usage, adequate sleep schedules, stress management, and amount of time spent on electronics (TV, computer, games, etc.) for non-work purposes. Because of the interconnectedness of these behaviors and their impact on overall health, the unhealthy behaviors can lead to poor health outcomes.

Behavioral Health

Mental health, substance use, and addictions are under the umbrella of behavioral health. There is a growing awareness of how behavioral health impacts and influences health outcomes. A nationwide opioid epidemic and a high rate of suicides are turning the spotlight onto discussions that were often swept under the carpet.

Mental health broadly covers emotional, psychological, and social well-being. How a person thinks, feels, and acts is all part of mental health. Aspects of daily living, including interactions with other people, decision-making processes, and dealing with stress are all influenced by mental health. A person can experience different levels of mental wellness over the course of a lifetime. Factors contributing to mental health problems include biological factors, life experiences, and family history. Biological factors are related to genetics and chemistry in the brain. Life experiences—whether being a spectator or the actual victim of incidents like trauma and abuse—also influence how a person thinks and acts. Family history is also a factor when patients have blood relatives with a history of mental illness.

Addiction is a condition in which a person uses a substance or has a behavior that provides an immediate, short-term, personal reward and compels the person to continue using the substance or repeating the behavior despite its negative, long-term consequences. Substances that are misused include alcohol, nicotine, prescription medications like opioids and other pain killers, and inhalants like paint, hairspray and glue. Examples of behaviors that can be addictions are gambling, shopping, eating, gaming, risk-taking, and exercise. A behavior becomes an addiction when a person goes to extremes as a result. Some impacts on a person of addition include:

- Struggling with physical or mental health issues like stress and weight loss or gain.
- Experiencing disruptions in everyday activities due to the behavior.
- Suffering negative consequences, such as the loss of home or job.
- Being unable to stop the behavior despite the negative consequences.

Addictions are often seen in patients that also have mental health issues. According to 2014 statistics by the National Institute of Mental Health, 20.2 million adults were diagnosed with a substance use disorder and 39%, or 7.9 million, had co-occurring mental health illness and substance use disorder.[4] The presence of either mental or addiction disorders can complicate the treatment of physical conditions and present challenges for patient interactions and engagement.

Within the context of behavioral health, the goal is recovery—which is rarely a linear process of continued improvement. The recovery process is a journey that can include stages of progress and relapse. This occurs along the line of the adage, "one step forward, two steps behind," meaning that it is not always a straight path with continual forward momentum. As with conditions like diabetes, the journey to recovery requires supports like personal motivation, assistance, and understanding from peers, friends, and family, finding the correct medications and dosage, and being aware of progress or relapse. Depending on the severity of the behavioral condition, a provider may need to refer the patient to others with specialized knowledge and experience.

When moving toward payment for outcomes, integrating the impact of behavioral health on physical health is incredibly important.

While the behavioral health conditions may present one set of challenges for treatment, another significant barrier to treatment is the stigma associated with behavioral health. Unlike those with physical conditions, people with behavioral health issues are often viewed as weak and are given advice like "pull up your bootstraps" and "just deal with it," minimizing or dismissing the symptoms the patient is experiencing.

Screenings

As part of an office visit, your review of symptoms should include asking mental health, addictions, and substance use questions. Several screening tools are available that can be incorporated into your EHR.

Many tools are available in the public domain and can be found using simple web searches. A number of screening tools can be found on the website of SAMSHA (www.samsha.gov).[5] When considering which screening tools to incorporate in your practice, discuss options with your EHR vendor to determine if the tool can be embedded in the medical record or otherwise collected for reporting purposes within the system. You will also need to consider the amount of time that is added to each visit to ensure the questions are answered. For some questionnaires, the patient may answer questions independently with the self-identified answers available to the provider. Be sure to have a process established that addresses the next steps when there is a positive screening.

The most commonly used depression screening tool used is the Patient Health Questionnaire. For a quick depression screening, providers can ask the two questions from the Patient Health Questionnaire-2 (PHQ-2)[6] to determine if further evaluation is needed. The questions are scaled on a four-point spectrum related to the frequency of experiencing issues:

A total score greater than three indicates that further screening is warranted.

TABLE 5.1   Patient Health Questionnaire-2 (PHQ-2)

Over the past 2 weeks, how often have you been bothered by any of the following problems:	Not at all	Several days	More than half the days	Nearly every day
Little interest or pleasure in doing things	0	1	2	3
Feeling down, depressed or hopeless	0	1	2	3

This questionnaire can then be followed up with additional questions from the expanded Patient Health Questionnaire-9 (PHQ-9),[7] which has a total of nine questions and uses a similar rating scale.

Scoring on the PHQ-9 indicates the level of depression as mild (5), moderate (10), moderately severe (15), and severe (20). The PHQ-9 can be used as both a screening tool as well as diagnosing, monitoring, and measuring the severity of depression.

TABLE 5.2   Patient Health Questionnaire-9 (PHQ-9)

Over the past 2 weeks, how often have you been bothered by any of the following problems:	Not at all	Several days	More than half the days	Nearly every day
1. Little interest or pleasure in doing things	0	1	2	3
2. Feeling down, depressed, or hopeless	0	1	2	3
3. Trouble falling or staying asleep, or sleeping too much	0	1	2	3
4. Feeling tired or having little energy	0	1	2	3
5. Poor appetite or overeating	0	1	2	3

6. Feeling bad about yourself or that you are a failure or have let yourself or your family down	0	1	2	3
7. Trouble concentrating on things, such as reading the newspaper or watching television	0	1	2	3
8. Moving or speaking so slowly that other people could have noticed. Or the opposite, being so fidgety or restless that you have been moving around a lot more than usual	0	1	2	3
9. Thoughts that you would be better off dead, or of hurting yourself	0	1	2	3

Substance use screenings can be focused on alcohol, drugs, or both. However, not all misuse of substances involves illegal drugs. Misuse can include behaviors like taking prescription medications or using household items inappropriately (paint, glue, hairspray, etc.). With screening, be sure to identify both legal and illegal substances. Two examples of simple screening tools are:

- CAGE-AID—a four-question tool with yes/no answers that addresses drug and alcohol use and can be used to determine if additional screening is needed.[8]
- AUDIT-C—a three-question tool with identification of quantity of alcohol consumption.[9]

Longer tools include the original AUDIT and DAST-10, both of which are 10 questions. AUDIT is focused on alcohol use and DAST is focused on drug use. [10]

Screening, Brief Interventions, and Referral to Treatment (SBIRT) is an approach that—as the name implies—screens, intervenes, and refers to treatment. The SBIRT model adds an intermediate step between screening and referral. This step involves showing the patient the risky behaviors and providing advice and feedback. [11]

Incorporating screening tools can help identify the unmet needs of your patients. The screenings may also help identify factors that could create barriers to improving their overall health. Developing cultural competency among your staff can help avoid misdiagnoses and unnecessary testing while providing a higher level of quality service.

Cultural Competency

Cultural competency is commonly thought to be offering language translation services or hiring bilingual staff that speak the language of your patients. While this can help bridge some communication barriers, cultural competency has a much broader definition. To be culturally competent, both the organization and staff within the organization need to be able interact effectively with patients and families/caregivers of different cultures. For these purposes, culture encompasses demographic and social characteristics as well as race and ethnicity. These characteristics can include:

- Age
- Gender
- Sexual orientation or identification
- Disability
- Religion
- Income level
- Education

Take a moment to stop and think about each of the defined characteristics. Cultural competency is so much more than race and ethnicity. Each of the above aspects influences the whole of a person. No one factor defines who that person is, or how they will act and react. There is a lot of attention on the differences between age groups (e.g., baby boomers, Gen X, Gen Y, millennials) with focus around work ethic

FIGURE 5.4   Cultural Characteristics

and value. Though you rarely hear this described as cultural differences, that is exactly what they are. Culture surrounds each person in many ways and often unconsciously. To be culturally competent, you need to understand the values, beliefs, and behaviors that are influenced by these characteristics and provide care that meets the individual patient's needs.

> **A common analogy about culture is to compare it to an iceberg.** With an iceberg, only one-tenth is visible above the water, with the larger portion hidden below the surface. Culture is very similar, with 90% of it invisible and easy to run into when you do not have a full understanding of its background. The shape of what is below the iceberg waterline is difficult to determine and the same is true of culture.[12]

With culture, visualize three levels:

1. The top level is what you see easily, the surface culture, like language, dress, gestures, music, and arts.
2. Below the surface are the strategies, goals, and philosophies that guide interaction—including how patient will interact with their own health.
3. The final level is deeply submerged and is an unconscious and unspoken level of basic underlying assumptions. These are beliefs and feelings that are taken for granted by members of the culture.[13]

As healthcare providers, these last two levels are where it is easy to inadvertently cross the line into areas where offense can be taken by the patient or family, and relationships can be broken. These unspoken and unconscious rules include the beliefs, motivations, attitudes, and communication styles of an individual. This aspect of culture influences how a person views and treats elders, youth, mental health, child-rearing, and tolerance of pain. It also affects how an individual handles emotion and sets standards for what is acceptable for personal space, physical touching, and eye contact.

Understanding these aspects of culture are important for gaining trust and building a strong relationship with your patient. Value-based care cannot succeed when the patient does not trust the provider.

To build awareness, the first step is to examine both your personal cultural characteristics and understand how your beliefs influence how you view the world and influence your interactions with patients and caregivers. Unconscious bias is another description for how your values, beliefs, and experiences may cause prejudice without intent or realization. When moving toward cultural competency, you need to be more aware of your own assumptions and how they may influence your interactions. Developing positive attitudes and respect for other perspectives are important in building a level of cultural awareness and competence. Differences will exist between your culture and that of everyone else, since each person is unique. The first stage of cultural awareness is to define your own frame of reference and understand how your culture has shaped your views, attitudes, and value.

The next stage is cultural sensitivity. In this stage, you acknowledge that there are differences and similarities between you and your patients. While some patients may have similar backgrounds and cultures as you, not everyone will, and being aware of this helps to build cultural sensitivity. This involves changing how you assess interactions with patients, as what you may view as acceptable and normal may be viewed as unacceptable to your patients or their caregivers.

Cultural competency is the final stage. To be competent is more than just being aware of cultural differences or tolerating those differences. The heart of cultural competency is developing awareness, skills, and knowledge. Critical thinking and reflection are applied to your own thoughts and what you think about how your patients and their caregivers view the world. Understanding characteristics about the patients you serve allows for a more targeted approach in learning how to better communicate and to consider how your personal views may differ.

The four pillars of cultural competency are:

- Awareness
- Attitude
- Knowledge
- Skills[14]

With communication, this includes both potential language barriers as well as how a person may express an issue. As an example, a Japanese patient may complain about abdominal, neck, or head pain. Providers and staff would find it helpful to know that within the Japanese culture, the abdomen, and neck are often the site for emotions. Pain in these areas may be an expression of depression, based on a study published in *Family Practice*.[15] Without an awareness and understanding of cultural differences, a significant number of tests could be ordered to rule out physical issues. The patient would not see improvement because the actual source of the problem would not be identified until all other possibilities were ruled out. While this is a common diagnostic approach, asking some additional questions may lead to a better understanding of the symptoms. Developing the cultural awareness, sensitivity, and competence to identify that not everyone will express, understand, or even acknowledge mental conditions helps patients receive needed care.

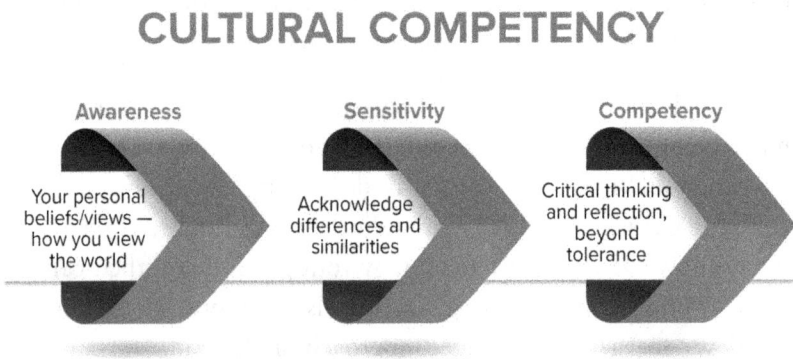

CULTURAL COMPETENCY

Awareness

Your personal beliefs/views — how you view the world

Sensitivity

Acknowledge differences and similarities

Competency

Critical thinking and reflection, beyond tolerance

FIGURE 5.5 Cultural Competency

To achieve cultural competency, each level of a practice, from staff to overall organization, must demonstrate awareness, knowledge, and skills. Competency is developed through openness to new experiences and learning, either through formal training or informal interactions. Some ways to learn more about being culturally competent include:

- Know the characteristics of your patient population to raise awareness of potential cultural differences.
- Hire people that live in the same communities as your patients and, if needed, bilingual staff.
- Use simple words and sentences and speak slowly. Do not repeat the same words or speak loudly when interacting with patients that have limited English proficiency; a lack of understanding English does not mean that the person cannot hear, so speaking louder does not help.

- Use people first language, which places the person before the disability or condition to avoid making the disability or condition what defines the person. As an example, rather than labeling someone a diabetic, the description is a person living with diabetes; this language is particularly important to individuals living with severe mental illness and those with intellectual or developmental disabilities.

- Pay attention to nonverbal communication, including eye contact, physical contact or touch, speech (loud/soft and formal/informal), personal space, and gestures like nodding, pointing, thumbs up, etc.

- Be open with your patients and admit that you may not be aware of cultural differences; you can ask for their guidance or feedback.

- Avoid making judgments and check your own personal assumptions.

- Embrace and celebrate diversity.

- Be empathetic and learn how a patient would like to be treated.

As a child, you may have been taught the golden rule, which is to treat others as you would want to be treated. This rule has evolved beyond the golden rule to be the platinum rule, which is to treat others the way they want to be treated. Bridge cultural differences and be able to interact effectively and consistently with everyone your practice serves.

A framework for documenting and implementing workflows and processes for cultural competency is the National Standards of Culturally and Linguistically Appropriate Services (CLAS). As defined by the U.S Department of Health and Human Services, the National CLAS Standards are intended to improve quality, advance the equity of healthcare, and eliminate disparities. CLAS consists of fifteen standards that cover the following topics:

- Principle standard–overall statement related to care and services

- Governance, leadership, and workforce
- Communication and language assistance
- Engagement, continuous improvement, and accountability.[16]

These standards define how the organization and its staff will act in efforts to eradicate healthcare disparities and improve quality and promote equality in health so that everyone can achieve the greatest level of health. By adopting the CLAS and developing specific workflows and actions, a practice or healthcare organization can demonstrate its commitment to improving quality of care and eliminating healthcare disparities.

Conclusion

To be successful in a value-based approach to care, you need to be able understand your patients at a deeper level than just addressing the presenting problem. Developing an awareness of culture, behavior health, and social determinants of health is a necessary first step for your practice. Promoting a deep understanding of your patients expresses the values of your practice and creates a strong relationship with your patients. These essential building blocks create an environment that encourages your staff and patients to address barriers to positive health outcomes. This deeper level of knowledge about your patients is used to redirect resources to move toward population health.

Chapter 6

Identifying the Biggest Opportunities to Deliver Value

As established in Chapter 4, a significant amount of data is currently collected every day by your practice. If your practice is using an EHR, this data is readily available to summarize information about your practice and your patients. Understanding who your patients are, the most prevalent medical and behavioral conditions, and the challenges of social determinants and other non-medical factors affecting care allows for managing population health.

With limited resources, your practice can use data and information about the patient population to stratify patients according to levels of risk. For practices with greater resources, implementing sophisticated analytics and reporting using big data techniques are possible. But smaller practices can also implement elements of population health without expending significant resources and breaking the bank. Understanding the basics of using data that is already available can help practices implement population management techniques on a small scale and reap the benefits of improving health outcomes. The basics include understanding sources of data, an overview of risk stratification and predictive modeling, and how to use the information to change how care is delivered.

One of the shifts your practice must adopt is an approach that incorporates the use of data in decision-making. This is a significant cultural change for many physicians and staff at the practice level. With meaningful reports, dashboards, or other representations of data, not only is the patient picture more complete, but so is the picture of your patients as a group of people treated by your practice. The best way to use the information available within the practice is to combine clinical and financial information. The greater the amount of information available, the better the analysis to determine how to allocate resources. This method assists in identifying which patients have a greater likelihood of realizing improvements in health and well-being. A practice can also use the data to determine the best allocation of resources by predicting which patients will benefit from additional services like care planning, coordination, and management.

Challenges Are Not Non-Starters

Value-based care is about delivering quality care while demonstrating that you have impacted care to achieve better health outcomes, lower costs, and/or enhanced the patient experience of care. The idea of using data to inform care may be a difficult concept to embrace, or it may already be a foundation for your practice. Either way, addressing the need for data, and using data within decision-making, is when conversations get even tougher. Issues with the availability of data, confidence in the reports, and sufficiency of resources are three challenges that need to be surmounted. The good news is that those barriers do not need to result in a stalemate for moving to value-based care.

Availability of data is a double-edged sword. Part of the issue is gathering the correct information while avoiding information overload. Your EHR is designed to collect information. Your vendor should have information available to connect what is seen on the screen by an end-user to the data element available in either a report or for extracting information in a text file (or another file format) that can be manipulated. If you are not able to determine the correct data field that matches information collected on user screens, contact your EHR vendor for assistance. The EHR vendor should be able to provide a partial data dictionary or other data mapping for key fields. The vendor is unlikely to disclose a full data dictionary or mapping of the system architecture, as this is considered proprietary information.

However, if you can identify a subset of data points, requesting similar information for the smaller set of information is a reasonable request. To identify the information you will need, the best starting point is to determine what information you would like to see as the output in terms of reports for alerts or other ways of using the data. Developing a clear picture of the final reports is also a way to avoid data overload. Understanding information needed to populate the report helps ensure that you gather the necessary information during patient interactions. Communicating and training about gathering certain data elements and requiring that the fields must be completed before the record is closed helps reinforce to providers the importance of documentation. When designing reports, consider how you may need to dive deeper into details or require more information than you initially visualize. Flexibility in how and what data is pulled is as important as the ability to manipulate the data.

Lack of confidence in reports generally stems from concerns about accuracy and completeness of data and will slowly erode the effectiveness of your benchmarks and data usage. These two detrimental factors are present when data fields are not mandatory and when training for providers on actual documentation and its importance has not been enough.

Incomplete and inaccurate data: When transitioning your practice, focus on being clear about why the changes are occurring and how documentation affects the final output.

As you move forward, staff and physicians need to capture as much information as possible. The goal is to avoid poor charge capture and can help with risk adjusted payments. In some cases, the activity may not be billable, but you may use certain codes to capture additional information.

> **Example:** As part of a visit, a depression screening is administered. This is captured in the medical record and the provider enters CPT© code 96127 to demonstrate that a depression screening tool was administered. Depending on your contract and billable codes, this may or may not result in a specific payment. However, documenting the code allows for capture that the screening was completed.

Another way to capture the use of a depression screening tool is to have a data field within the EHR where a clinician can input the specific score based on the screening tool results. If your depression screening tool is the PHQ-2, your providers would record the score from the tool. This score can then be used with other information, like a specific diagnosis, which allows you to see how many patients screened positively or negatively. This is particularly important when you are looking for data about chronic conditions like diabetes or COPD. Depression or anxiety is often present in chronic conditions. In analyzing data about your patients, you may find comorbidities. The behavioral health conditions impact the mental health and well-being of your patients and may be a barrier to improving health outcomes.

If you find that is an issue for your practice, you may want to add resources that address the behavioral health needs of your patients to achieve better overall health outcomes. Or if you are comparing patient characteristics among different physicians, you may notice a trend that depression and anxiety are not being identified properly if a physician has a high number of individuals with chronic conditions but no patients with comorbid depression or anxiety.

Staffing and financial resources for IT and data analysis tend to be another barrier cited against moving to value-based care. Larger practices and health organizations are likely to have the financial resources available to support a data warehouse or other big data solution with dedicated IT and reporting resources. Small to medium-sized practices may not have the resources to dedicate to managing the data and creating reports. Looking for external support or including this as a responsibility for administrative personnel is possible. Screen for this skill when hiring new staff or identify an existing staff member that would enjoy learning a new skill. Training on how to use Microsoft Excel does not need to be expensive. Starting small and working with a limited amount of information is better than not starting at all.

Do not let data crunching be a barrier—use of data is essential under value-based payment programs.

Data Sources

Sources of data include information collected in the practice management and clinical modules of the EHR, external information incorporated into the patient record like labs, tests, and images, as well as information gathered from the patient or sent by a health plan payer. A challenge with having multiple data sources is determining where information is located within the systems, extracting the data, combining it into a user-friendly deliverable, and finding ways to generate meaningful reports.

Having the analytical skills and supports necessary to make meaning of the information and create actions may be lacking, particularly in smaller practices. The primary source of information, the EHR systems, were not originally created with population health management considerations in mind. EHR systems were initially designed to improve documentation, support billing, reduce manual recordkeeping, and allow for better access to patient information. Several EHR vendors have moved in the direction of expanding their systems to manage population health. But the process can still be cumbersome and information difficult to obtain. If your EHR does not have reporting features to allow for population health management, one option for addressing this issue is to extract information from the EHR. Big data

FIGURE 6.1   Data Sources

options are available using extracted data that is generally stored in a data warehouse and harnessed to sophisticated analytical programs and reports. Or for a simpler option, your practice can create reports and dashboards to summarize meaningful data in Microsoft Excel.

Stratification

To manage a patient population, you need to categorize your patients into groups to allow for a tailored approach to meeting their needs. This is known as stratification. To stratify a patient population, create groups based on assessed level of risk. Elements to consider in defining risk are high costs or utilization, or an elevated chance of negative outcomes, such as admission to a hospital or death.

Despite the challenges, your practice can start small and use the information currently available within the clinical and practice management modules to assess the overall needs of patient population. In reviewing information pulled from your system, the goal is to determine where your practice has the best opportunity to affect change and help patients improve their overall health. Knowing your baseline for current health outcomes and the characteristics of your patients helps identify which patients may need additional supports. These supports include creating care teams, developing care plans, identifying additional resources within the community, creating closer partnerships between primary care and specialists that address needs, and offering targeted education and outreach, to name a few.

The stratification is used to tailor the outreach and care management focus for the patient population. Focus on creating three risk categories—low, medium, and high risk. Depending on the size of your practice and the resources available, the number of people being

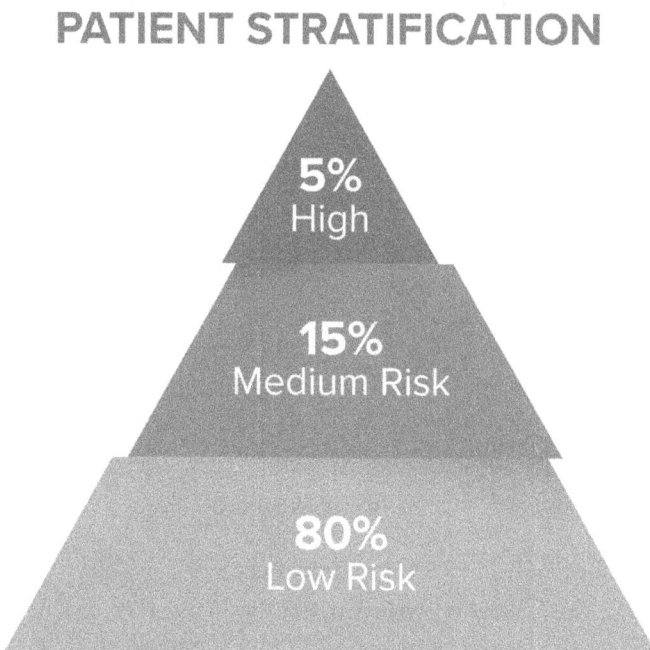

PATIENT STRATIFICATION

5%
High

15%
Medium Risk

80%
Low Risk

FIGURE **6.2** Patient Stratification by Risk

managed with a higher level of support will need to be less than 10 to 20% of your patients.

In a primary care population, approximately 80% of all patients seen can be grouped into a low risk category. These are the routine care patients seen for acute illness unrelated to a chronic condition, or for check-ups and immunizations. When looking at patients overall, many individuals in treatment are likely in a mode of prevention and wellness. The primary focus for these individuals is to ensure maintenance of health and well-being. Limited resources are allocated to this group as these patients need minimal support or outreach. Most outreach to this group is for reminders such as annual wellness visits, recommended vaccinations, good nutrition and exercise behaviors, as well as general education related to health.

Primary vs specialty: In theory, all the patients treated in a specialty practice have been identified as needing a higher level of care. For a specialty practice, the stratification needs to be tailored to your specialty and *how* you define risk. Your patient population may also include patients that are in stable condition with good control of their condition (like an endocrinologist with patients that are maintaining good blood sugar levels). Your outreach may be geared toward education about medications, reminders about medication refills, and how to determine when contacting the office is necessary.

Once the 80% of low risk population has been classified and removed from consideration, the practice can then focus on the 20% of patients that have higher level of needs. These remaining individuals will be classified as either high or medium risk.

Those identified as medium risk representing about 15% of your patients. Of the patients grouped as medium risk, focus on those individuals in the upper portion of this risk category. It is interesting to note that of the patients that generate the highest cost in any given year, only 30% were also in the higher risk categories in the prior year. This means that a larger percentage of people (70%) were either medium or low risk. This is part of the reason for focusing on individuals that could be considered medium risk. These are individuals that are at risk for developing a chronic disease, recently diagnosed, or otherwise in the early stages of a chronic disease. Also included in this group are individuals that have been diagnosed with a chronic condition but are relatively stable.

The high-risk category should be 5% of all your patients. In reviewing total costs, the general rule is that 5% of all individuals generate the highest costs and a large percentage of all costs (in the range of 80 to -90% of all healthcare costs are generated). These high-risk-categorized individuals are highly complex and have a higher probability for acute or adverse conditions. Generally, patients with the highest risk classification have demonstrated high costs, poorly controlled or complex conditions, multiple inpatient or emergency room admissions, or are diagnosed with more than one chronic condition.

These individuals are often already identified by payers and are receiving support and management by the health plan. While seemingly counterintuitive, this group may not warrant a significant allocation of your resources. Your practice will want to cooperate with the health plan and others involved in the patient care, but individuals in the high-risk group may already be receiving multiple supports. If that is not the case, then dedicating more resources may have a greater impact. The issue with this group of individuals is the complexity of cases and usually the involvement of multiple people or organizations in managing care. Establishing a clear understanding of who is the lead in managing care of the high-risk population is essential, as is understanding your role. Care coordination is a stress point within the healthcare system and is generated in part by lack of communication.

Some payers provide information about individuals at risk for developing chronic conditions or who present an elevated risk for generating high costs or utilization in the future. These individuals also represent a group of people who should be considered for more intensive support and management. Despite whatever complaints you may have about your payers, most health plans have significant analytical resources that utilize predictive modeling to identify individuals at risk for higher costs and utilization. These analytics are also used to inform approaches to outreach, allocation of resources, and management of members in programs like disease management and intensive care management. Information may be provided by the health plan as a report related to gaps in care.

Predictive Modeling

Predictive modeling is based on statistical modeling and is used to identify high risk individuals by forecasting future utilization and expenses. Health plans have employed this methodology for many years. Providers in health systems and ACOs are also tapping into models to identify high-risk individuals. Because the models rely on historical data, a wide range of data is included, like claims from providers, facilities, ancillary services, and pharmacies. Models are built on the assumption that the past predicts the future. While there can be some variation in the accuracy of predictions, algorithms that are based on a wide set of data can reliably predict an increased risk or higher probability of adverse events.

For example, if the model was predicting individuals at risk for developing type 2 diabetes, data points related to individuals already diagnosed with type 2 diabetes are analyzed to develop statistically valid correlations between factors. Based on analyzing all available and relevant data, certain factors are identified as indicators that a person is at risk for diabetes and used to create assumptions. A model is then created based on the assumptions and insights the data have provided. This model is then tested against older data to test the validity of the assumptions. If the validity exists, then the model is used against current data to predict who may develop type 2 diabetes in the future. Predictive modeling may rely on pharmacy data as an early indicator of the presence of the developing chronic conditions. This makes sense, because often the first step is to prescribe medication to address the condition that is not improving.

After identifying individuals that are at risk for developing a chronic illness or having an acute episode, interventions are crafted. For a health plan, these interventions may include patient outreach and education or alerting the treating physician. At the practice level, you may also provide outreach and education or place an alert on the patient record to discuss nutrition and preventive measures that can be taken.

Regardless of what the model predicts, clinical judgment is *never* replaced. The predictions and predictive modeling should be considered as an additional clinical decision support tool. Based on the relationship and interactions of the clinical team and patient, the physician or other member of the care team may be aware of changes in patient behavior that are not being captured in predictive modeling.

Example: If a patient is identified as being at risk of developing type 2 diabetes because of a higher blood sugar level, the predictive model would not know if the patient has made significant changes in behavior, such as modifying eating habits to avoid sugars and minimize high glycemic foods, and successfully maintaining an exercise regime. The physician and care team, however, would know about these changes in behavior. In this case, the practice may lower the risk scoring because of more current information or other information that is not in the algorithm or model.

Leaving a higher risk classification in the example above is not an issue. This allows your practice to verify that the patient maintains the new eating and exercise habits. If your practice is interested in predictive modeling, additional research is warranted. Models are not static and need ongoing evaluation of accuracy and validity. Your organization will also need to evaluate if purchasing support is more cost effective than building and maintaining in-house capability.

How to Stratify Your Patient Population

Even without developing predictive modeling capability, your practice can benefit from stratifying your population and creating new workflows to administer care based on identified risk levels. Your stratification of patients is designed to assign a risk score to each patient based on the specific complexity of the patient. In creating risk stratification classifications, a complex classification system is not needed. Using a simple assignment of low, medium, and high risk works well and is easy to manage. You may want to even consider adding a fourth category of medium-high to address the patients that fall in the top of the medium category. One option is to use a modified LACE tool for stratification.[1] The LACE tool requires information related to usage of inpatient and emergency department services. The scoring assesses length of stay for a current inpatient admission, acuity of admission, presence of comorbidities, and number of emergency room visits (LACE).

While complex risk stratification methodologies exist, most of the systems and designs are not affordable to practices that are not part of a large health system or group practice. Any size practice can analyze patients at a high level and assign a risk classification based on the priorities of your practice. Use either internal data, or referrals, and any other information available from external parties like a health plan or other payer.

Internal Data

The practice can also create a registry, which is another way to group patients. Registries are often used in practices to identify patients that meet certain criteria. Generally, the registry is simple to run, with the end user identifying specific variables that describe the patients. For example, if the practice is focusing on individuals with elevated blood sugar levels, a registry or report is created that shows individuals with an A1c score greater than 9 and have a diagnosis of diabetes. To take this example further to illustrate stratification, assume that the practice is only focusing on diabetes as the sole factor in determining risk and that the stratification will be based only on A1c scores. The classification groupings would be defined as high risk if blood sugar is greater than 12, medium-high risk is 9-12, medium risk is 7-9, and anyone below 7 is low risk. The practice would then run a report that shows the A1c score for everyone in the practice. Based on each person's A1c level, a stratification level would be assigned. With each of the classification groups, the practice would identify how the approach to care is tailored based on the stratification.

For patients without an A1c test result, the practice would need to determine how to classify the group. Creating an additional group of "unknown" may make sense if the practice worked to eliminate the category by reminding patients to complete the blood test.

While the diabetes classification is a simple example, the concept is the same as you expand the criteria and add complexity to the classification. Depending on the level of complexity that can be incorporated into a registry, you may be able to use registries to identify and classify patients into risk stratification groups.

Otherwise, extracting data from the clinical and practice management modules may offer better information, particularly in looking at the global characteristics of your patient population. Gathering the following information can provide a wealth of insight about your patients:

- Demographics
- Insurance payer
- Diagnosis or diagnostic grouping, allowing for multiple diagnoses to determine co-morbidity
- Procedure codes

- Lab test results
- Vitals like blood pressure, weight, height, and BMI
- Number of medications
- Date of the last office visit
- Date of next scheduled office visit

Using even the minimal information above, your practice can gather a basic snapshot of the existing patients. With the data, you can answer questions like the following:

- What are the top diagnoses?
- What are the top five to ten procedure codes?
- Are the appropriate lab test results available given a specific diagnosis?
- How many patients are diagnosed with more than one chronic condition?
- How many patients are diagnosed with a medical chronic condition and a behavioral health condition like anxiety or depression?
- Are there differences in the data when split out by season, ZIP Code, race/ethnicity, age, gender or other factors?

Depending on the practice's available resources, the analysis can be handled within a reporting function or even manipulated in Microsoft Excel.[2] Being able to look at different variables allows for your practice to gain an understanding of the patient population from a global perspective, rather than using registries that narrow the focus immediately. After gaining a broad understanding, the registries can be used to identify patients that meet the criteria that you have established as most relevant.

External Data

Certain external data can also be helpful in assessing your patient population. Gathering this information may be challenging, but the endeavor always strengthens your practice's data operations.

Access to information about admissions and discharges of your patients from your local inpatient hospitals and emergency departments is pivotal. In some areas, this information may be available through a health information exchange (HIE) or ADT (admissions, discharges and transfers) data files.[3] With the HIE, you register patients as being attributed to your practice, after which information about the patient's admission or discharge can be sent. In the absence of an HIE, your practice may be able to negotiate for information to be sent directly to your practice by your local hospital. Health plans are also a resource for ADT information. Depending on the size of your practice, a manual form with a small number of patients may manageable. However, the best way to receive this information is through a data exchange. This will require a unique identifier, like a patient identification number, to connect the data elements.

In some areas, however, a practice may find that the hospital either does not have the resources to share this information or competitive practices prevent the hospital from being transparent with the information and disclosing it. This creates a challenge as data from an HIE is only as good as the comprehensive participation by providers, payers, and ACOs that are submitting data to the HIE. The HIE also relies heavily upon accurate information being entered within the system. If the HIE is working and functioning well within your community, you can gather a significant amount of information related to your patients and their activity.

Depending on your payers and local ACO or health systems, your practice may receive reports or data directly from these external parties about the patients in your practice. This information is likely to be summarized and may identify individuals that a health plan has stratified as a higher risk. Consider this information in your stratification approach as well. The information that is provided by these types of entities may provide a broader picture of what is occurring with individual patients. Because a payer, health plan, or ACO is paying claims across the health care system, their data will have better information related to activities and services that are provided to your patient outside of your practice.

The challenge with the information provided by payers is that often you need to log into a portal to gather patient information. Each payer has a separate portal and the ease of use and availability of actionable information will vary. This process is labor-intensive and not integrated with the patient record. However, for your higher risk patients, gathering information from the payer and incorporating that data can help refine your stratification and provide insight to achieve greater outcomes. Information that is useful to gather includes admission and discharge dates for inpatient and emergency department stays, discharge diagnoses, medications, and length of time in facility. Payer reports show gaps in care that may also provide insight related to specific patients. Tapping into this data allows your practice to identify individuals that are incurring high costs, have unplanned inpatient admissions, and frequent visits at the highest levels of care.

The end goal is to use the best available information to understand who your patients are and the underlying characteristics of those patients. There is no one right way to stratify risk and classify your patients. Each practice will identify unique characteristics and what patients need the greatest amount of time and attention to achieve better outcomes. Depending on your current EHR, your practice may be able to create stratification categories, which can help direct resources appropriately. Based on your analysis of patients, specific patients can be identified in the EHR as belonging to a stratification category based on your definitions. Once a patient is tagged to a stratification classification, the system should then allow for alerts. This creates a heightened awareness that a different level of communication and treatment are needed when the patient arrives in the office or is proactively contacted.

Interventions

After the stratification is complete, the approach to care, including level of support to be provided, can be crafted for each stratification level. For the lowest risk level, your practice might focus on prevention and education with low-cost outreach such as e-mail for communications through the patient portal, or possibly even automated messaging or traditional postal mail. Some practices even post generalized health tips to social media based on things like common chronic conditions in their practice population and data collected from low-risk stratifications.

For the stratification level that had medium- to medium-high-risk patients, the approach to care may include different screening tools and a more tailored delivery of services. With this risk classification, interventions are more targeted, and the patients receive not only education and encouragement but also additional support for managing care, setting and measuring goals in a care plan, and fostering self-management skills. The patient stratification also dictates how you allocate your resources.

PATIENT STRATIFICATION

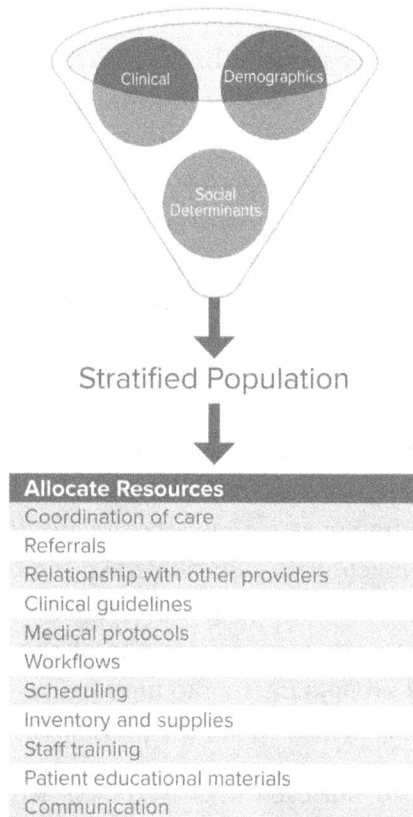

FIGURE 6.3 Patient Stratification Leads to Resource Allocation

Generally, the patients classified as medium- or medium-high-risk is the category where you can make the largest impact. This is not meant to imply that the high-risk category should be ignored. Your practice still needs to help these individuals improve health and realize better outcomes. But if your stratification aligns with that of the health plan, you may find that the patient is already receiving assistance and support. Health plans often focus on patients with the highest risk and those at the top of the medium-risk category. The health plan, and possibly the local hospital, are likely to have resources monitoring and outreaching to the patient. Supporting the health plan or hospital is important, but the effort needs to be coordinated and should not overlap with other targeted interventions.

Duplication of services: In the larger picture of the overall patient health, the goal is to avoid duplication of services and to use the available resources most effectively. Because health plans focus on the higher cost/higher utilization patient, the practice may or may not see a reduction in the cost of treatment for the patient. Sometimes savings are generated from avoided future costs or reductions in utilization and cost from another part of the health system.

In creating interventions for the practice, consider what resources are available. Every practice must consider resource constraints, whether the constraint is funding or staff time. The practice information system should automate as much work as possible. An example of automating work is to create a letter campaign for outreach. If your practice identified the lack of a mammogram as one of the indicators of your medium or high-risk group, targeting to increase the number of women that complete a routine mammogram is a preventive measure.

After drafting an outreach and awareness letter, an automated email can be sent to each patient can be programmed into the system and sent via the patient portal for patients identified as not having a mammogram within the specified time frame. Using the patient portal to e-mail the letter saves a significant amount of time and money when compared to using postal mail. The savings include not only the time to address each envelope, add postage, and mail the letter but also the supply cost of the paper, envelope, and stamp. Another way to automate an outreach task is to set automated calls as a reminder for upcoming visits and include information related to the preventive measure.

An outreach campaign to individuals with certain risk factors can be effective. Registries can be run to identify patients that meet certain thresholds even though the person may not be classified as high risk. Some examples include:

- Patients not seen by your practice within an appropriate time frame, i.e., three, six, or twelve months (this will depend on your specialty).
- Individuals that have not had recommended general preventive measures such as immunizations or screening such pneumococcal vaccine or colonoscopy.
- Individuals with a particular diagnosis that have not received all preventive services, i.e. individuals diagnosed with diabetes that have not had a foot exam within the last two years.
- Individuals that have used tobacco products in the past (possibly a higher risk).

Care Management

With the highest risk patients, establish a clinical team to focus on helping the patient manage his or her condition through care planning and with support of care management. This clinical team performs not only outreach and education, but also helps the patients set goals to achieve and sustain behavior change.

If your practice is unable to perform a detailed analysis of the patient population, some examples of high-risk patient registries that could be managed include:

- Individuals who have poor control of conditions, i.e., elevated A1c levels greater than nine.
- Individuals who have used tobacco products in the past.
- Individuals who are diagnosed with substance use disorder or serious mental illness condition.
- Individuals who are diagnosed with a complex condition.
- Individuals who have more than one chronic condition.
- Individuals who have high usage of emergency room, inpatient, labs, tests, and readmissions to the hospital.
- Individuals who are prescribed multiple medications.
- Individuals who have significant barriers to care due to social determinants of health.

The list above also identifies factors to consider when performing a detailed analysis of your patient population. With your high-risk patients, a written care plan is created based on the input of the patient combined with the medical expertise of the clinical team. The care plan incorporates the needs and preferences of the patients when establishing treatment goals. The identified goals include functional goals that are meaningful to the patient. When the patient specifies a goal, engagement is increased because the goals are something that the patient wants to do, or at least is willing to do.

When creating goals and discussing options, examine any barriers to achieving the stated goals. These barriers may be physical, emotional, or social. Documenting these barriers and options for overcoming the barriers within the care plan helps the patient remove the barrier. The care plan also includes a problem list, expected outcomes, and information to manage medications. The care plan is to be updated based on specific dates, with appointments scheduled for reviewing progress. Revisions to the care plan also can occur outside of regularly scheduled updates as needed.

The written care plan is printed and given to the patient as a reference. Having the plan available in the patient portal is also useful to some patients. The care plan helps the patient stay on track with behavior changes and achieving goals, whether associated with nutrition, exercise, adherence to medications, or logging specific information into journals. Including a self-management plan provides additional tools and resources for the patient. This plan should include instructions on how to handle daily challenges and identify when the person may need to seek additional assistance.

One self-management tool that patients diagnosed with chronic and complex conditions may find useful is the Wellness Recovery Action Plan® (WRAP®).[4] Although the WRAP® was developed to address the needs of individuals with mental health issues, the reflective journaling can be used by anyone. The WRAP® is listed as an evidence-based program and practice. The plan is self-described and includes a daily maintenance plan which identifies tools and things that the patient might need to maintain wellness. The plan also walks through triggers such as events, activities, people, or special dates—and allows for identifying early warning signs when adherence to the plan is breaking down. The plan also documents what happens when a crisis occurs and allows for advance directives.

Narrowing Your Focus

The delivery of value-based care requires the use of data to demonstrate improvement in outcomes and care. Your practice collects a wealth of data that can be harnessed to help allocate resources. Narrowing your focus helps to avoid informational overload. Understanding your patient population, stratifying level of risk, and tailoring outreach and interventions is accomplished by knowing the characteristics and needs of your patients.

CHAPTER 7

Structuring the Practice

Aligning your resources to achieve and demonstrate outcomes requires that your practice be structured to meet comprehensive patient needs and deliver the best care possible. Your practice must facilitate access to appointments, as well as clinical and general information, through your scheduling practices, and offer options other than traditional office visits. Examples include telemedicine, phone consults, and group visits, to name a few. Value-based care is also delivered when evidence-based care guidelines are used, and a comprehensive assessment and medication reconciliation are performed.

Access to Care

In a patient-centered healthcare model, access to care is defined as having services available based on what is preferred by the patient. This means having office hours available at times that are convenient for the patient, and that the patient can receive care when needed. With the introduction of urgent care centers and retail clinics, practices are facing competition in the delivery of services from new entrants to the healthcare community. Their competitive advantage is convenience.

In today's fast-paced society, people are less willing to wait and more demanding in requesting to be seen by a physician when they feel it is necessary. Providers will not retain patients if patients cannot be seen on a same day basis for acute needs. This does not apply only to primary care. Specialty care also faces challenges with wait times, particularly for new patient appointments. Wait times for new patient appointments often range from three to six months. During this waiting period, the condition of the patient may degrade, resulting in a visit to the emergency room—which leads to higher costs, a potential decrease in health outcomes, and a longer period to improvement or stabilization of the condition.

In addition, access to care can impact continuity of care. While providers might believe that clinical competency is the main reason why a patient remains or leaves—this has been disproven. Delivering

COMPONENTS OF ACCESS

FIGURE 7.1   Components of Access

customer service through readily accessible appointments is becoming even more important in a world that is plugged-in 24/7.

One of the objectives for Healthy People 2020 is to ensure access to healthcare services.[1] This includes having appropriate insurance coverage and access to healthcare services that are geographically convenient. Access is defined as having a healthcare provider that the *patient* trusts. A lack of trust creates a barrier to patients accessing care. Developing a strong relationship between the patient and the provider involves building a foundation of trust and being able to communicate.

When access to care is missing, the system experiences higher utilization—which drives up costs due to unnecessary care. By ensuring that patients can be seen in a practice setting, the system prevents conditions from becoming emergent. This helps to avoid acute episodes that result in hospitalization or using an emergency room for non-emergencies and preventable illnesses and conditions. By maintaining access to a personal physician, whether in primary care or with a specialist, the patient is better engaged through a meaningful relationship with the physician or care team. The patient is also more likely to comply with, and adhere to, recommendations of a trusted physician and care team. The entire office acts as a team and influences the patient perceptions about trust and respect. Bridging the relationship between the patient and the team is discussed in Chapter 8.

When patients do not have access to healthcare, greater complications occur as well as difficulties in gaining control of chronic and acute conditions. The patient may experience stress and anxiety when seeking specialty care to confirm or negate a diagnosis. The unknown, particularly for a life-changing condition, causes significant stress and emotional distress. In some cases, the stress of the unknown and the waiting period to find out results is often worse than the experience after a diagnosis. At least with confirmation of a diagnosis, the patient can start addressing alternatives. This is particularly important when looking at wait times for the patient to be seen in specialty care. If the patient does not believe that care will be provided in a timely manner, the patient may choose to seek services at the emergency department, again creating higher utilization and cost as well as potentially generating a backlog in the emergency department for care that could be treated in another setting.

Scheduling

To address issues with access, practices have been encouraged to adopt open access models. In an open access model, the volume of appointment types is not fixed. The schedule accommodates appointments as needed, based on the total hours available rather than the number of available appointments by appointment type. Moving to a full open access model has been difficult for many practices. An alternative is for your practice to retain appointment availability every day for same day appointment scheduling.

Traditionally most practices maintain schedules where specific appointment types are established and only a certain number of specific appointment types are scheduled in any given day. Because of the limitation on the number of available appointment types, a patient may wait for a longer period than expected.

To review access to services within your practice, start by evaluating the current schedule and scheduling procedures. The goal of evaluating your schedule is to define the supply or total hours available for seeing patients and to understand this availability by provider and by the day of the week. In your scheduling procedures, identify the days of the week that your practice is open, the normal office hours of the practice by day, and each provider's availability to see patients (defined by day of the week and appointment types). The normal appointment types are then associated with an estimated "normal" time increment. When these factors are combined, total available hours for a given week can be determined. This is known as the supply. In an easy example, if one provider has available 7 hours a day with two new patient appointments (60 minutes), four 30-minute visits and twelve 15-minute visits, the total availability is 7 hours a day.

Assuming the same schedule for 5 days a week, the total supply for the provider is 35 hours and 80 appointments.

A standard metric to determine access to services is the third next available appointment. On a routine basis, your practice should evaluate the amount of time until the third next available appointment for each appointment type. If you measure this weekly, you would measure the total number of days between the date of measurement and when the third opening for that appointment type exists. If you are measuring the time for a new patient appointment and the measurement date occurs on January 2, you review the schedule to determine the three next available appointments. Assume that the available appointments are January 15, 23, and 31. The wait time for the third next available is 29 days (the difference between January 31st and January 2nd). Some practices may already be aware of access issues through use of tools like maintaining a waiting list. Tracking requests for appointments provides insight about patient demand. Analyzing past appointments and comparing what was identified as available versus what appointments were scheduled and delivered will identify patterns in demand and potentially about supply as well.

When participating in value-based programs, easy access to appointments is partly how your practice can reduce overall costs, generate savings, and improve outcomes, including the patient experience. Within current value-based programs, two metrics of interest to health plans and other payers are:

1. Reducing usage of unnecessary and preventable care in emergency departments and hospitals.
2. Access to follow-up care within 7 days of discharge from an emergency department or hospital, as required by applicable HEDIS measures (discussed further in Chapter 11).[2]

To achieve these two metrics, your practice must treat patients promptly. To facilitate access to appointments, your practice needs to define availability standards that state the acceptable amount of lapsed time by appointment type. For example, a primary care practice may set acceptable times by appointment, like new patient appointments within 7 business days, follow-up care post discharge within 2 business days, and wellness appointments within 14 business days. With defined standards, your practice has set goals for appointment access and availability. To help meet these standards, leaving unscheduled blocks of time on a regular basis can alleviate wait times. These blocks of unscheduled time are utilized for urgent needs. This is a form of modified open access scheduling.

Another commonly utilized option to explore is the use of clinical teams. Rather than scheduling with only a physician, patients are seen by a member of a clinical team that may not be the primary physician or provider. By using additional members of the clinical care team, more appointment availability and flexibility is offered to your patients that need assistance. As discussed in the next chapter, an important aspect of using a team is that the patient develops a relationship with each member of the team. The members of the team must share all pertinent information about the patient interactions with other team members. The sharing of information is critical to the success of the team, otherwise the patient does not feel that the team is aware of his or her needs and is required to repeat information. Not keeping team members in the loop is obvious to the patient, discredits the team concept, and does not foster trust with the patient. In worst-case scenarios, patients leave the practice feeling like their questions and health issues were not addressed.

Insights about access and availability can also be gained by tracking cancellations and gathering reasons for the cancellation. Reviewing patterns in canceled appointments, particularly for those with advance notice, can shed light on patterns for why appointments are canceled. The actual number of patients that routinely cancel appointments tends to be a small percentage. When gathering information about cancellations, create an easy tracking system using codes that offer general groupings like transportation, unexpected conflict, work, sick family members, childcare gaps, etc. Explain to the patient that information is being requested about the cancellation so that your practice can track data for evaluating access. This approach helps avoid eliciting a defensive response from the patient.

Examine cancellations by the appointment type. Interestingly, the reasons for cancellations and no-shows may differ by appointment type. If a pattern evolves where follow-up visits are routinely canceled, your practice may want to evaluate procedures for scheduling follow-up visits for factors like amount of lapsed time between appointments. If a patient is scheduled for a follow-up visit but does not feel that the appointment is necessary, the patient may cancel or not appear for the appointment. Office visits to receive lab test results are a prime example. If a patient has lab work after an office visit, evaluate if a follow-up appointment is necessary. This is particularly true when the lab results indicate no concerns. Requiring a patient to be seen to communicate this information is an example of volume-based, not value-based activity. While the office visit generates a billable activity, the downside is that the appointment could have been scheduled for a patient that truly needed to see a provider. Also, the patient is inconvenienced when information could have been communicated remotely.

For patients that have a pattern of cancelling or not showing for scheduled appointments, consider combining as many services as possible within one visit. By avoiding having the patient return to the office for a future visit, cancellations and no-shows may be reduced. Bundling services in one day includes preventive services or other routine matters even when scheduled for acute illness or other needs. This is contrary to how practices tend to function. Normally, the patient needs to fit into the appointment structure of the allotted time for the appointment and provider's calendar. This approach should be tested on a small number of patients to ensure that the schedule is not entirely disrupted. The practice does not want to create large, unused blocks of time. The open access model can also help with bundling services into a longer appointment because of the flexibility in removing constraints by appointment time. Bundling services can lead to better outcomes.

Also, with a change in the reimbursement model, the focus remains on providing necessary services and not on whether all the services will be paid as allowable because they were performed during one office visit.

Alternatives to Office Visits

Being able to receive clinical advice both during and after normal business hours helps alleviate access issues. A patient may be able to receive assistance and have questions answered by speaking with a nurse or other practitioner. Telephonic triaging can assess whether clinical advice by phone is appropriate or if the patient must be seen in the office. The rapid growth of telehealth shows that patients like engaging in their health in this way.

To meet patient needs and preferences, your practice can offer both telephonic and electronic access. Many EHR systems offer a patient portal. The patient portal allows for two-way communication between the patient and provider. Rather than a patient needing to call or be seen in the office, a patient can use the portal to ask questions, schedule visits, or request a prescription refill. Not scheduling a face-to-face visit also offers an opportunity for questions and concerns to be answered by someone other than the physician, if the person is acting within the scope of license or they are handling issues that do not require a clinical license.

With the shift to value-based payments, the pressure to require a face-to-face visit is reduced, leading to greater access and addressing patient needs without regard to whether an opportunity for a billable service is being missed. This has the added benefit of expanding the responsibilities of your staff and creating another level in the relationship between the patient and your practice.

Another alternative to create greater access is utilizing alternative technologies or group visits. Telehealth is the most prominent alternative technology. Telehealth is broadly defined as using electronic information or telecommunications to support the delivery of healthcare without face-to-face, immediate proximity. The definitions for telehealth vary, and state and federal definitions may differ. Telemedicine is another term often used in conjunction with telehealth. Telemedicine is generally defined as delivering a clinical service whereas telehealth can involve non-clinical services such as providing education. In the context of this material, the term telehealth is meant broadly and includes both clinical and non-clinical services. Telehealth is particularly important in rural communities and other areas where access to specialty care and other services is limited.

Telehealth offers the opportunity for the patient to be seen by a remote provider, and overcomes barriers associated with transportation and geographic availability. Additionally, offering telehealth is an option for delivering services outside of traditional office hours. Online visits offered outside of traditional office hours are gaining in popularity and offer convenience to patients. Ways to deliver telehealth include live video and "store and forward." Live video involves two-way communication with real-time interaction through technology like a smart phone or tablet app with online access. "Store and forward" involves collecting and recording information to review later. The distinction between live video and "store and forward" is the timing of the exchange of information. Live is in real-time and "store and forward" is not.

Two other telehealth mechanisms are remote patient monitoring and mobile health technology. With remote patient monitoring, patient data is tracked from the patient or other location and sent to the practice or provider. The patient information is collected on a regular basis. On the provider side, alerts are established to identify when patient data indicates a problem or concern. An example is having glucometer or blood pressure readings sent each day either by the patient entering information or automated technology transmitting the readings through a wearable device. With a glucometer reading, the patient and/ or the practice receives an alert if blood sugar levels are too high or too low. If the patient is notified, they can be educated to determine what actions to take or instructed to contact the care team when readings are outside the acceptable range. Sometimes the practice receives the alert and reaches out to the individual patient to determine next steps. These could include the patient being directed to continue monitoring blood sugars, to visit the office for a face-to-face evaluation and assessment, or, if life-threatening, to seek immediate help by calling 911 or going to the nearest emergency department.

Mobile health is an area where new applications are being created daily. Health-related apps can regularly record measurements, allow a person to set reminders, offer access to educational information, and track a treatment plan for routine care. The number of health-related apps available is tremendous. Depending on the resources of your practice, the mobile health information collected by the patient can be gathered through electronic data submission on a regular basis and utilized in an office visit in place of a manual log to provide an update on patient progress.

Lastly, to manage demand for appointments without expanding office hours or adding additional staff, your practice can examine how services are utilized between primary and specialty care, or among specialists. The goal between primary care and specialty care is to ensure that the patients are being seen and managed at the most appropriate level, and by the most appropriate provider. For specialty care, practices evaluate if any patient can be managed by primary care. Transitioning stable patients to primary care offers the opportunity for your specialty care practice to provide faster access to new patients or people needing the depth of experience that a specialist provides.

Similarly, primary care practices should ensure that patients treated within their practices are appropriate for care and treatment and only refer patients needing more advanced or specialized care. When a patient is involved with multiple specialists and primary care, care coordination is critical to ensure appropriate care and prevent overlaps or gaps in care. To ensure the proper coordination between providers, service agreements define the flow of communication as well as roles and responsibilities. This topic is covered in greater detail in Chapter 8.

Evidence-Based Care

Evidence-based care is the combination of research-based evidence, clinical expertise, and patient values and preferences. The use of published clinical guidelines incorporates evidence supported by research. Clinical expertise references the sum of a clinician's experience, education, and clinical skills, and is a critical component of evidence-based care. Evidence-based care does not follow clinical guidelines without exercising clinical judgement or incorporating the patient's perspective. Using evidence-based care requires communication between patient and provider, or the patient perspective cannot be incorporated.

The goal is for the patient and provider to decide upon the appropriate course of treatment action as a team. Through the patient-physician relationship, the provider needs to explain the best practice—including the source of evidence and why the treatment is considered the most appropriate course of treatment. When jointly developed goals are the result of shared decision-making, patient engagement tends to be increased, which can lead to better compliance and adherence with recommendations and in turn, better health outcomes.[3] The importance of communication and additional techniques are addressed in Chapter 9.

To promote best practices and align your infrastructure to deliver quality care, providers in a healthcare organization must maintain current knowledge on the latest medical research and clinical practice guidelines. Maintaining that knowledge can be challenging given the sheer volume of clinical practice guidelines. Currently, over 1,000 clinical practice guidelines are published. Each medical society maintains clinical practice guidelines that are most relevant to their membership, and many other organizations publish guidelines as well. Nationally, the clinical guidelines are placed in the National Guidelines Clearinghouse and managed by AHRQ. The clinical guidelines are compiled from research that examines whether treatment works. A benefit of the guidelines is that they are based on information collected from more patients than any one physician could possibly examine and treat. Physicians, and other providers, benefit from this broader range of collective experience.

To ease and facilitate the use of clinical guidelines, incorporating the clinical guidelines into the EHR is recommended. When the guideline is embedded in the EHR, the workflow can be designed to alert the care team or physician to review the guidelines. The alert is intended to help the provider and reduce errors by displaying the relevant guideline. Incorporating the guidelines eases the burden on the provider to maintain current knowledge about the latest research. As a point of reference, a physician would need to read at least seventeen articles a day for a year to read all the current literature and research related to primary care guidelines—an overwhelming task. Strategically using your EHR and technology can reduce the burden when workflows and training support new knowledge.

Comprehensive Assessment and Medication Reconciliation

As discussed in earlier chapters, understanding the whole picture of your patient as a person allows for identifying needs and preferences of the patient—as well as potential barriers to improving and maintaining health and wellness. While most assessments cover the patient and family history, expanding the assessment to include a review of factors associated with behavioral health and social determinants of health provides additional insights.

When considering social determinants of health, your practice can consider aspects of where a person lives, works, and plays—and how those factors influence the patient's ability to maintain a healthy lifestyle and manage his or her health. Characteristics of family and cultural values also influence health outcomes. As described in Chapter 5, collecting this information in the patient record allows for a full capture of patient background and history. This also allows for information to be included in the analysis of the patient population for purposes of identifying needs.

Gathering information about communication needs and understanding the level of health literacy of the patient and caregiver also impacts your ability to influence health outcomes. Think about a person that may be considered a moderate risk for poor health outcomes due to slightly elevated blood pressure or blood sugar levels, while being mildly overweight. While changing eating habits and incorporating some exercise may help the patient lose weight and reduce blood pressure or A1c levels, consider what might be the difficulties for that patient if support at home is lacking, access to healthy food is limited, or income prevents the person from purchasing healthier foods. Knowing this information allows for a different discussion about goals and overcoming barriers. Rather than instructing the patient to change eating habits and increase activity, the discussion involves talking about the challenges to incorporating those two changes into daily life.

Unhealthy behaviors, as well as mental health and substance use, affect the ability of people to manage conditions and maintain healthy lifestyles. Including a review of these during the health assessment can lead to identifying additional issues that need to be addressed. Another source of information to consider during the assessment is patient reported data about health status and obstacles to managing health. Incorporating questions about health and lifestyle factors or functional status surveys like the 12-item Short Form Health Survey (SF-12) allows your practice to gather a broader set of information than focusing solely on the acute need or presenting problem. Outcomes are geared toward improving health as well as the patient experience. Addressing needs from a whole person perspective increases trust by communicating an understanding of challenges and further engaging a patient to be motivated to adopt necessary changes in his or her lifestyle.

Lastly, as part of each visit, reconciling all medications helps reduce contraindications and errors. Although most providers request information about medications, many patients do not understand to include not only prescribed medications but also over-the-counter medications, supplements, and herbal therapies. Including questions about all types of medications as well as supplements and herbal therapies provides a more complete picture. Entering this information into the EHR helps your providers to educate the patient and prevent errors.

Delivering on Value-based Care

Delivering patient-centered care supports the achievement of outcomes that drive value-based payment mechanisms. Meeting the needs and preferences of your patients requires access to service and care as needed, and when convenient for your patients. The convenience factor extends not only to availability of appointments but also to how your patients interact with your practice. Additionally, gathering a wide variety of information about your patient allows for a broader understanding of factors influencing the ability to maintain a healthy lifestyle or improving health and wellness.

Gaining knowledge about barriers from social determinations of health and historical or current presence of unhealthy behaviors, mental health conditions or use of substances by the patient or family members provides deeper insight about the patient. This information is gathered as part of a comprehensive assessment and is combined with medication reconciliations and evidence-based practices to deliver optimal care and encourage better health outcomes.

Changing the infrastructure through processes and workflows to support this approach is only one part of the equation. Ensuring that your providers and staff are structured and encouraged to participate in a team-based approach to care is how you deliver on value-based care.

CHAPTER 8

Incorporating Team-Based Care

As defined by the National Academy of Medicine, team-based care is the provision of health services to individuals, families, and/or their communities by at least two health providers who work collaboratively with patients and their caregivers—to the extent preferred by each patient—to accomplish shared goals within and across settings to achieve coordinated, high-quality care.[1]

It is an approach that does not yet come naturally in the modern healthcare setting, but discussion taking place across the industry indicate it can change things for the better.[2345] Reports from organizations that have implemented team-based care are positive, suggesting it leads to lower turnover[6] and reduced rates of burnout.[78]

The Case for Team-Based Care

Depending on your environment, making the case for team-based care may be a tough sell. Nonetheless, it is turning out to be a pivotal piece of the pay-for-performance puzzle.

Reasons for moving to team-based care are to:

- Improve the quality of healthcare.
- Expand access to care.

TEAM-BASED CARE

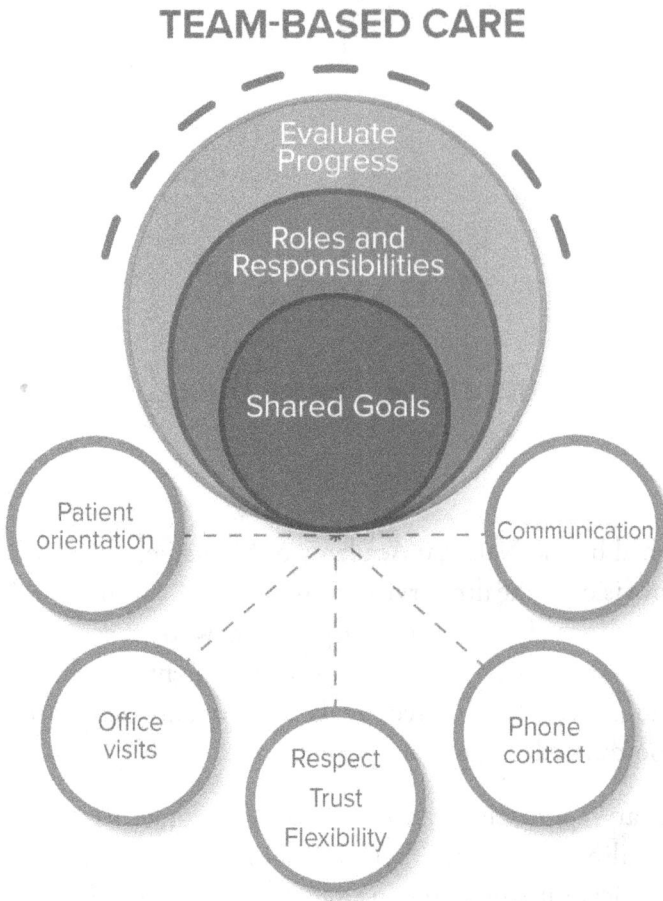

FIGURE 8.1   Team-Based Care

- Take advantage of specific skills and expertise of each team member.
- Match specific roles to the abilities of each person.
- Provide a more effective and efficient way of delivering care to patients.
- Strengthen relationships with patients by having deeper and broader connections with the office.
- Increase job satisfaction for physicians, nurses, and staff, resulting in less turnover and burnout.

Workforce Shortage

Statistics showing anticipated shortages in healthcare are staggering. According to the Association of Medical Colleges, the physician shortage is projected to range from 42,600 to 121,300 by 2030.[9, 10] The demand for nurses is projected to increase; with current demand growing 15% and expected to jump 28.3% by 2030.[11] The impact and timing of retiring baby boomers is not yet known, which adds unpredictability to the estimates. The anticipated shortages are not just in clinical positions. In an MGMA poll from May 2018, 61% of organizations identified a shortage in qualified applicants for non-clinical positions within the past year.[12]

Turnover amplifies the effects of the workforce shortages. The costs of recruiting and training a new employee for a practice or healthcare organization are significant. Costs projected by the *Journal of Nursing Administration* are $82,000 to replace a nurse, which does not include the cost of onboarding and training. For physicians, the numbers are even greater.[13] Physician turnover can cost from $400,000 to $1 million between recruiting costs, lost revenue, and start-up expenses.[14, 15] Even with other members of a practice, the cost of turnover can range at least 20% of annual salary and upwards to 150-200%.[16] Retention of staff must be a priority for every practice.

Burnout

One of the drivers of employee turnover is burnout. Burnout results from long-term emotional and physical stress experienced by physicians, nurses, and other workers in healthcare. Burnout sufferers doubt the value of their work and competence. The cost of burnout is not just seen in turnover but also in the actions of those experiencing burnout who try to push through it.

Burnout can result in:

- Increased medical errors
- Higher turnover
- Decreased patient satisfaction and quality of care

- Elevated risk of malpractice incidents (and related increases to insurance premiums)

Burnout can be experienced by anyone in the practice. For physicians, initiatives have been implemented by different physician associations due to the prevalence of burnout and associated suicide rates.[17] Physician suicide rates are higher than the general population. Suicide rates for women physicians is 2.27 times greater than for the general female population and, for male physicians, the rate is 1.41 times greater.[18, 19]

Reasons for burnout can be grouped into categories of organizational and individual factors. The organizational factors are generated by the work environment and culture, along with the policies of the organization and practice. Individual characteristics are inherent to each person and how stress is handled.

From an organizational perspective, some factors that influence the likelihood of burnout include:

- Quick pace and high energy required all the time
- Dysfunctional work group, including negative personalities and micromanaging supervisors
- Lack of control over schedule
- Unclear roles, responsibilities, and job expectations
- Practice not aligned with skills and interests
- Lack of clearly defined values and mission or a mismatch in what is stated compared to actions
- Lack of delegation and trust to accomplish tasks

In general, individuals that work in healthcare are likely to suffer from burnout due to the nature of being in a helping role. Personal characteristics of physicians and nurses will amplify the likelihood of burnout. The characteristics include:

- Conditioning of education (this is particularly true for physicians).

SIGNS AND SYMPTOMS OF BURNOUT

Exhaustion	Detachment	Lack Drive
Drained or constantly tired	Sarcasm and cynicism	Feeling incompetent
Change in appetite	Disengaging and isolating	Lack of purpose and motivation
Irritability or anxiety	Negative talk to self/others	Sense that nothing matters

FIGURE 8.2   Signs of Burnout

- Putting the patient first without work-life balance.
- Coping with the stress of dealing with sick and dying patients.
- Having a high tolerance for stress (over time, chronic stress affects the body and mind.
- Needing to feel in control.
- Having perfectionist traits.

Stress awareness should be addressed on a regular and consistent basis, and, remember, April is stress awareness month and presents an opportunity for targeted education. Having an engagement program to reduce stress benefits your practice and reduces turnover.

Implementing a team-based approach allows a practice to structurally reduce stress by connecting individuals and their roles to their strengths and interests, promoting a sense of unity, allowing delegation, and maximizing each person's potential.[20]

Avoiding burnout means controlling and reducing stress. Your practice can aid individuals experiencing burnout by supporting the individual and by changing the environment of the organization. As an organization, your practice can lessen the risk of burnout.

- Know common stressors and triggers.
- Help staff and physicians to find the original, or new, meaning in their work.
- Encourage work-life balance and a healthy lifestyle.
- Assist staff in connecting personal values to responsibilities and the organizational mission.
- Offer professional help.
- Aid staff in connecting with co-workers for positive support and encouragement in the workplace, and friends and family outside of work.

Organization-Level Supports

When building a team, the individual team members should complement and contrast each other. Select team members based on individual skills, the ability to offer different perspectives, and willingness to work together. Creating a team requires having not only the correct number of people but also a blend of skills on a team, supported by leadership. Carefully considering the initial care team composition is critical.

These are some pivotal questions to ask potential team members when building a cohesive team:

- When and how do they prefer to give and receive feedback?
- What is their preferred method of communication?
- How do they prefer to disagree?
- At what time of day do they feel most productive?

Team members alignment or lack of alignment on these core characteristics can mean success or failure.

As an organization, the team needs to have support for initiatives and the ability to act independently. As your practice is moving toward team-based care, assess the skills of existing personnel, look at hiring practices, promote training, and ensure that evaluations of performance and related incentives are aligned with the goals of team-based care.

BUILDING THE RIGHT TEAM

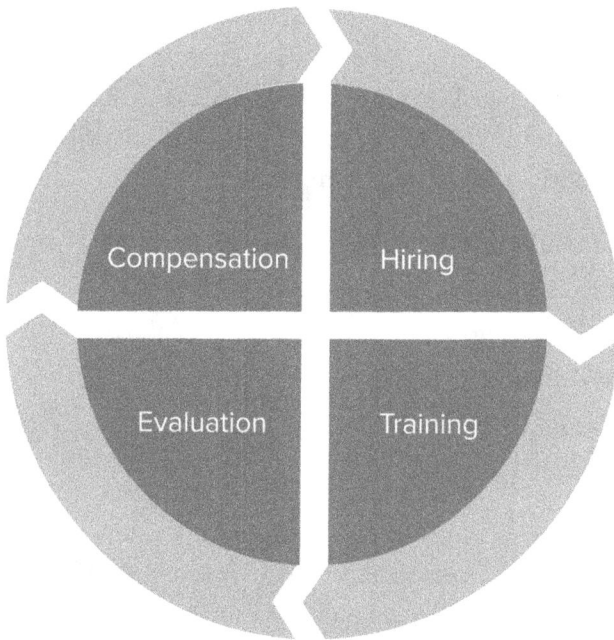

Compensation

Hiring

Evaluation

Training

FIGURE 8.3   Building the Right Team

Hiring

Shifting to a team-based model may require your practice to examine hiring policies and procedures. Job descriptions must be updated to reflect the values and characteristics required to participate in the team. When screening new applicants for positions, evaluate the candidate's personal values for alignment with both organizational and team values. While technical or clinical skills are important, so are having the right attitude and willingness to be a part of a team. Ideally the applicant will show a desire to help, be creative, focus on resolving problems, and potentially be able to deal with intimidation. With a team approach, staff members may be asked to stretch beyond what have been traditional roles.

Training

When moving to team-based care, training can ensure that the team and entire staff have the new skills that are needed. Educational materials that focus on team-based care are widely available online at no cost, including at Learning from Effective Ambulatory Practices (LEAP)'s www.improvingprimarycare.org. Some key skills and examples of topics to consider as part of training are:

- Communication
- Dealing with conflict
- Teambuilding
- Cross training
- Cultural competency
- Emotional intelligence

Other types of training can include on-the-job training where a person is shadowing a coworker to learn, or role-play where each person takes a turn at being different members of the team. Role-playing can be very eye-opening and is a unique opportunity for team members to understand how other people view their behaviors and roles. Use training as a way of developing problem-solving and leadership skills while encouraging creativity. Incorporate cross-training and backfilling into the team's processes. Be sure to have fun in the training. A positive environment reduces stress and helps keep attention and focus on priorities.

Building a strong team is a primary goal of the training. Because of the shift in how the practice functions, work to establish that each person understands the team, how they fit into the team, and the skills and strengths of each team member. Be clear and reinforce these ideas with training and supporting documents like job descriptions and performance expectations.

Evaluate progress

Each team evaluates progress by looking at both advancement toward goals and team function. When the shared goals of the team are developed, one strategy to use is SMART goals.[21] Progress is easier to evaluate when you are establishing goals using these as an approach.

GOALS NEED TO BE:

Specific

Measurable

Assignable

Realistic

Time-related

FIGURE **8.4**   SMART Goals

The goals are measured based on the time frames identified within the care plan. Also, measure other aspects of the goals, such as whether the person assigned to the goal completed it and fulfilled the assigned roles.

Patient satisfaction is both a formal and informal measure of team functioning. Patient satisfaction surveys can be adjusted to capture details about patients' experiences with team-based care. In the survey, ask about team-based care, including relational components such as feelings of rapport, being listened to, and that their input is welcome. When patients can affirm those experiences, the team has successfully included them in the care plan.

Tools are available to help assess team effectiveness,[22, 23] but broadly it is demonstrated by:

- attendance at team meetings,
- helpfulness which can be measured among members of the team including the patient,
- efficiency in resource use,
- initiative in taking ownership of any issues that arise and working to creatively solve problems,
- quality outcomes based on identified measures and goals,
- interaction and communication among team members,
- making sure that the documentation reflects all activities,
- managing conflict,
- making sure that everyone's voice is heard by allowing and encouraging different perspectives, and
- accountability by completing assigned role and responsibility.

Providing administrative support so the team can set goals and feel supported in achieving them may be the most important piece of all. Successfully implementing these adjustments will take time and ingenuity, but the payoff is life-changing for everyone involved.

Performance evaluations

Performance evaluations can consider not only individual performance but also the performance of the team as a whole. By evaluating team performance, your practice reinforces the importance of working together on a team and achieving collective goals, not just individual goals. Some elements to consider in a performance evaluation are:

- Attendance and participation in team activities
- Progress and achievement of goals
- Resolution of conflict
- Helpfulness and initiative
- Patient satisfaction scores

Sharing the results of outcomes and patient satisfaction scores are great ways to demonstrate how the team is performing. By sharing those metrics with all team members, the communication facilitates the team identity and provides an opportunity for each team member to consider what he or she can do differently to improve performance.

Implementing a Team-based Care Program

One of the key steps is deciding who among your patient population should be served with this model. As described in Chapter 6, your practice will have built out its stratification approach and can use that information to identify patients that will benefit from team-based care, primarily those in the medium to medium-high risk brackets. The practice may choose to pilot its first team-based care program with a subset of their patient population. The team then develops written care plans for treatment that reflect patient preferences and priorities. To develop a comprehensive care plan, the clinical team should include the characteristics outlined in Chapter 5: social determinants of health, behavioral health, and cultural competency as well as medical conditions.

In a care plan, specific goals are established. As part of the process, specific team roles and responsibilities are defined to achieve the care plan goals. Part of the care plan will include communicating critical information with the patient, such as understanding who to contact, how the team will meet the needs of the patient, or in some cases, identifying where needs cannot be met. Care plan tools are available online, including the National Institute for Children's Health Quality (NICHQ) care plan template.[24]

Some needs of the patient are outside of the scope of what your practice can accommodate. In these instances, the clinical team connects the patient with other resources and then coordinates care.

Team Roles and Responsibilities

Team members must understand their specific responsibilities, or the team will fail. Team roles may be filled by a physician, nurse, and other clinical and non-clinical staff.[25] Job descriptions must articulate specific roles on the care team.[26] The responsibilities for any given clinical team member may differ from their traditional roles within the practice. An example is when a medical assistant is responsible for coordinating education, including directing a nurse to deliver certain education. *Harvard Business Review* reports that clear roles improve collaboration among teams.[27]

In defining roles, current activities assigned to specific job functions may not change but responsibilities could expand after defining specific roles. For example, within the clinical team, internal staff members need to be assigned to specific functions such as:

- **Leader**—responsible for guidance of the overall care team.
- **Care coordination**—working within the healthcare system to ensure overlaps between settings and providers do not cause fragmentation.
- **Education**—can cover a wide variety of information including medications and self-management tools.
- **Medical or clinical expertise**—assessment and treatment options with knowledge of best practices in evidence-based medicine.
- **Documentation**—ensuring that all information associated with a care plan and other relevant information is captured and accessible by all team members.
- **Administrative coordination**—insurance coverage, updating demographics, and verifying eligibility.[28]

One way to identify the specific responsibilities of a care team is to map the workflows associated with both a routine office visit and a complex visit.[29] The start of the workflow is either inbound contact by the patient calling for an appointment, or by outreach from your practice. When looking at the workflow, map activities of both internal staff positions and the patient. When the workflow is fully documented, each activity is linked as a responsibility that becomes part of team member job descriptions. If the workflow does not appear to include the patient, team-based care is not being delivered. Although a job description for the patient is not appropriate (no matter how much we might wish it was), your practice should provide a simple document defining patient expectations and responsibilities as part of a care team.

When applying this concept, keep in mind that multiple teams are present within a practice. Teams include the internal clinical teams that are generally grouped around a primary provider, the care team which includes the patient, a team that consists of other providers from the outside of the practice, and a full office team if the entire office does not participate as part of a patient-centered clinical care team.

Every team will go through the development process and it takes time. One well-known model for explaining team development is Tuckman's forming, storming, norming, and performing. Using training can help facilitate a team through these four stages, defined below.

- Forming
    - Members are unclear about roles and the skills and strengths of each person, and ground rules need to be established.
    - Members assume a level of formality, treating each other with polite distance, depending upon how well they already know each other.
- Storming
    - Members still view themselves as individuals, not part of the team.

- o Members may resist leadership and experience an increased level of conflict and emotion.
- Norming
  - o Members understand and are comfortable with individual roles.
  - o The leader of the team is seen as effective.
  - o The team starts to be cohesive and engaged.
- Performing
  - o The team operates autonomously and resolves issues well.
  - o The environment is open and trusting. [30]

Team meetings

Allow the team to have meeting time outside of the daily workflow. The team needs to be able to meet independently to review progress and continue with team development. Even after the team progresses through all stages of team development and is at the performing stage, the team needs time to maintain its identity, expand communication, and review how the team can be improved. By allowing time for team meetings, members have a chance to think through issues and concerns and even creatively brainstorm about new ways to perform as a team. This dedicated team time can also be used to recognize efforts and celebrate successes of the team.

Patient Orientation

Be prepared that with the introduction of team-based care to provide a patient orientation. A pivotal purpose of the orientation is to explain how care is different. Restructuring patient onboarding for those patients will need to involve everyone. The patient must understand the importance of his or her role and responsibility within the team. The practice can provide information to encourage the patient to disclose his or her full medical history, as well as care provided outside of the practice. The patient should be informed about the use of evidence-based care and the importance of self-management.

146

Introductions are another important aspect of the orientation process. Each person of the care team shares his or her name and what role he or she fulfills. The practice should also address communication needs, not only related to language but also preferences related to methods of communication such as phone call, e-mail, or text. Health literacy is another aspect to cover during the orientation. This can prevent or mitigate information from being misunderstood by the patient.[31] How the patient wants to participate in the care team is also important to gauge during orientation.

The orientation builds a base for strong communication between the practice and the patient, setting the tone for team interactions. Continue this communication and confirm patient participation at each encounter.

Communication

Strong communication strategies are required in team-based care. Internal communications, external communications, and communications with the patient must all be mindfully managed.[32] This requires awareness and the ability to look at other perspectives.

Communication skills are essential for a team. Information must be provided in a timely manner, but also in way that can be understood by all members of the team. One way to help the team prepare for patient visits is to have a quick meeting either once or twice a day, the team huddle.[33] Keep the huddle as a "standing meeting" to avoid the tendency to take longer than necessary.

When considering the needs of the patient as a part of the clinical team, consideration should be given for both preference of communication as well as patient literacy. Understanding and acting on the patient's communication preferences reinforces the team concept and builds trust. While verbal communication is essential, all information should be documented. As the saying goes, "If you don't document it, it didn't happen."

One choice a patient may make is to not be an active participant. Patients must have the choice of not actively participating.

Building Trust and Respect

As the practice fosters these values in their teams, the teams will connect and grow. Embodying the values and exhibiting strong communication skills will build trust with the patient and among the team members.

CHARACTERISTICS SHARED BY TEAMS

FIGURE 8.5 Characteristics Shared by Teams

Effective teams share defining values and characteristics. Some values that are important in a team are:

- Respect
  - demonstrates that each member of the team is valuable and contributes to the team;

- ○ is reflected in how information is communicated and how each team member is treated; and
- ○ acknowledges and embraces what each person brings to the team.
- Trust
  - ○ allows for reliance on other team members;
  - ○ is supported by transparency;
  - ○ is shown in honest and genuine interactions;
  - ○ is built by sharing goals, decisions, errors, and uncertainty;
  - ○ requires taking ownership of responsibilities;
  - ○ is demonstrated by helping others; and
  - ○ acknowledges that the end goal must be accomplished.
- Flexibility
  - ○ is shown by being open to new ideas and exploring options creatively;
  - ○ embodies the concept of continuous improvement;
  - ○ requires understanding that there is no one "right" way; and
  - ○ acknowledges that being constructive and innovative helps solve issues and meet goals.

A team develops its own rules and culture—which illustrates the need for values to be clearly identified. Values shape culture and create rules, both formally and informally. Each person on the team needs to respect those rules and culture. The team thrives in an environment that encourages open communication. It will be worthwhile to incorporate communication skills training and team building into the practice culture in anticipation of adopting team-based care.[34] [35]

Building Engagement at All Levels

In a time when healthcare is experiencing significant workforce shortages and an increased rate of burnout of physicians, nurses, and other healthcare workers, team-based care offers many opportunities to address causes of employee dissatisfaction and disengagement.

In team-based care, members of the team are encouraged and supported to function at the highest level possible whether in terms of license or responsibilities. The team has shared goals, has clear-cut roles and responsibilities, and involves the patient. Communication, trust, and respect are needed for a team to be successful. Understanding how to involve patients in teams and evaluate progress of team goals will likely involve additional training to incorporate new skills or expand existing skills. Building a team requires excellent communication skills and should be addressed as a topic of training. Inside the practice, the methods of hiring, training, and evaluating team members can be structured to facilitate team development.

How all staff, including physicians, are treated is essential to the viability of your practice. Engage your staff to understand the fundamental change in how the business and delivery of healthcare is evolving. When effectively engaged, your practice benefits by being more competitive in attracting and retaining physicians, nurses, and other clinical and administrative staff.

CHAPTER 9

Being a Part of the Community and Involving the Medical Neighborhood

Having made a commitment to patient-centered care, you need to consider where the practice fits into the larger picture of the community. Your practice needs to align with other practices, facilities, hospitals, or residential settings involved in the patient's care. Different patient needs require different partnerships. One critical part of performing well in a valued-based care program are wrap-around supports that ensure coordination as a patient moves within the healthcare system.[1]

Care Coordination

The current healthcare system is largely fragmented, with only rudimentary coordination between providers caring for a patient. Complicating the fragmentation is the fact that patients will often seek specialty care without informing all parties involved. When a patient has an unplanned admission to higher levels of care through either an emergency department or inpatient unit, there can be poor communication upon discharge. The patient may not be connected to the necessary follow-up care in an ambulatory setting, which can lead to readmissions or adverse events.

Care coordination involves the process of helping patients navigate through the healthcare system. AHRQ identified over forty definitions for care coordination and similar terminology. Based on that review, AHRQ created a common definition of care coordination; this definition is one of the most widely promoted:

> Care coordination is the deliberate organization of patient care activities between two or more participants (including the patient) involved in the patient's care to facilitate the appropriate delivery of healthcare services. Organizing care involves the marshaling of personnel and other resources needed to carry out all required patient care activities and is often managed by the exchange of information among participants responsible for different aspects of care.[2]

Care coordination is a role and responsibility of the clinical care team. Funding a dedicated care coordination position is easier when part of a large group or health system but can also be part of any proposal to move into value-based payment programs. How to approach a payer to fund new positions is discussed in Chapter 10, which is about getting paid to deliver outcomes.

If your practice moves forward with care coordination, patients that have comorbid conditions are most likely to benefit from this approach. Some studies show that focusing on the individuals with more than one chronic condition may reduce costs, thus reducing the funding that your practice would need for care coordination and implementation of a clinical care team.[3] This reduction in cost would be a benefit to a payer which justifies paying for the care coordination.[4] But more than any cost savings, care coordination has been shown to improve the quality of patient care and patient outcomes.[5]

As your practice moves to coordinating care of patients with chronic conditions, well-defined written agreements among the providers are pivotal. When a patient is involved with more than one provider, one of the first items to address is primary responsibility for patient coordination. Often this responsibility rests with primary care, but it does not need to be, and should be based on patient preference. If it is clear which practice is responsible for the coordination and the patient is aware of that, coordination can be handled by any type of provider.

As part of the care coordination role, the needs and goals of the patient should be assessed and shared among the providers. A single plan of care is developed. Goals are shared not only with the patient but also among the providers. Reaching a shared care plan that reflects input from all providers may require broad agreements that specify how the providers work together. This broad agreement can be followed with individualized agreements for patients with complex care plans. With a patient-centered approach, each provider involved in the care of the patient should be working toward the same goals. All parties involved in the care of any given patient should be aware of the total picture. This means knowing who is involved in care, how care is being coordinated, and how information is shared. This also means that the patient is engaged, understands the alignment, and knows how to work through the system.

When looking at workflows, your practice needs to consider and define how information will be shared with all directional flows identified. For most items, the information will have bi-directional flow. Information to consider when mapping workflows includes:

- Tests
- Images
- Lab work
- Transitions between care settings
- Care plans and goals

Ideally, the information will be shared electronically with data being exchanged directly into medical records, if shared systems are not available.

Transitions between care settings is an area where coordination of efforts leads to better outcomes and demonstrable savings for payers.[6] When a patient has been in a facility and is transferring back to a community setting, the level of support decreases. Ensuring communication while the patient is in the facility is ideal, but coordination must happen at discharge. Being alerted through either accessing the HIE or setting up systems for receiving notice of ADTs is pivotal. When discharged from a hospital or rehabilitative setting, the patient should connect with primary care and any specialist that plays a significant role in the patient's care. All providers should obtain a copy of the discharge summary, if access to the full patient record is not an option. Your practice must then incorporate this information within the patient record. The process of identifying and participating in transitions becomes part of the daily workflow, with information easily accessible and actionable.

Behavioral Health

A person's ability to think, feel, and relate to others is affected by their mental health. Individuals that have a chronic disease are likely to also suffer from depression. Below are some statistics from the CDC showing the co-occurrence of major depressive disorder with other chronic conditions:

- Cardiovascular 17%
- Cerebrovascular 23%
- Diabetes 27%
- Cancer 42%[7]

According to the CDC, the cost to treat individuals with chronic diseases is about 75% of total national healthcare expenditures.[8] Blue Cross Blue Shield (BCBS) produced a report noting that clinical depression has increased by 33% in its population between 2013 and 2018, with an average cost of $10,673 per person per year. Nearly 30% of people with depression have four or more chronic conditions.[9]

Behavioral health services have gained more focus recently.[10] There is a growing awareness and appreciation of the integral role that behavioral health plays in promoting positive outcomes. The presence of mental health or substance use disorders substantially complicates treatment and increases the cost of care. Efforts to control costs, particularly in Medicaid and with dually eligible Medicare/Medicaid beneficiaries, have drawn greater attention to the need to address behavioral health.[11] In order to integrate physical and behavioral health, specialty mental health providers are moving toward behavioral health homes.[12, 13]

Mental illness and mortality: On average, individuals suffering from depression die 9.7 years earlier than those without depression. Even more alarming is that individuals diagnosed with serious mental illness have a shorter lifespan by nearly 25 years. Between 2001 and 2017, suicide rates nationwide increased by 31%, with over 47,000 deaths attributed to suicide in 2017.[14]

As a medical practice, you need to be able to address the behavioral health needs of your patients. When looking at coordinating care and addressing the needs of your patients, the providers in your practice need to understand how behavioral health needs can be met.

It can be difficult to find a behavioral health provider that can quickly treat a patient.[15] Behavioral health practices are also experiencing significant workforce shortages. An initial assessment may easily exceed two months, with additional delays if the assistance of a psychiatrist is required.[16] The behavioral health system consists of a range of providers that limit their practices based on insurance coverage, specific employee assistance programs, or self-payment requirements. Individuals that have been diagnosed with a serious mental illness, serious and persistent mental illness, or serious emotional disturbance are more likely to be treated in specialty mental health systems, which tend to be distinct from the general medical community and other behavioral health providers.

Another challenge for behavioral health is the distribution of technology. Behavioral health providers have not received the benefit of government initiatives to assist with funding the implementation and use of electronic health records. The vendors offering EHR systems geared to behavior health are behind the rest of the marketplace in developing systems that facilitate workflows and manage outcomes. Many EHR vendors do not offer functionality that allows for documenting both medical and behavioral conditions within the same system.

To address the integral role behavioral health plays in managing overall health and wellness, practices are looking at co-located or integrated behavioral health services. The end goal is to review a patient's condition without differentiating between physical and mental concerns.

Models of Behavioral Healthcare

Behavioral healthcare must be evaluated based on what makes sense for your practice.[17] The best outcomes have been seen with an integrated model. However, some practices may not be ready for an integrated model and may start with the co-located behavioral health arrangement. Other models that are utilized are collaborative care and reverse integration.

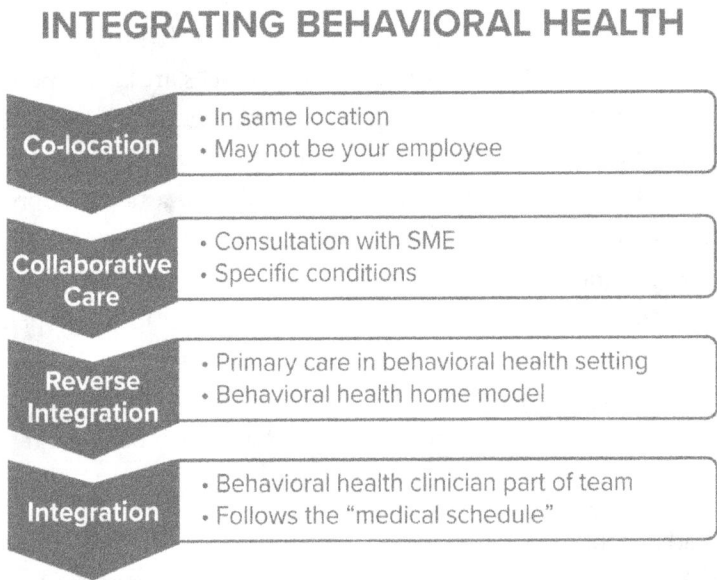

INTEGRATING BEHAVIORAL HEALTH

Co-location	• In same location • May not be your employee
Collaborative Care	• Consultation with SME • Specific conditions
Reverse Integration	• Primary care in behavioral health setting • Behavioral health home model
Integration	• Behavioral health clinician part of team • Follows the "medical schedule"

FIGURE 9.1   Integrating Behavioral Health

Co-Location

Under a co-location arrangement, behavioral health services are delivered in the same location as a primary care practice, but under the type of schedule that currently exists in the behavioral health system. This means a behavioral health provider sees 6 to 8 patients a day for traditional counseling in a 45- to 50-minute visit, or more patients if group therapy is provided.[18]

The behavioral health provider can be employed by the practice or be completely independent. Depending on the employment situation, medical records may or may not be shared. The largest patient benefit of having behavioral health services available in the same location is that stigma is reduced, and referrals are easier to facilitate.[19] While this is likely the easiest model to adopt, the integration is minimal and desired outcomes may not be achieved.[20] The care is still separated, and information may only minimally be shared.

Collaborative Care

The collaborative care model is generally a consult model.[21] Medical providers consult with a psychiatrist or other behavioral health provider regarding individuals that have been diagnosed with specific conditions that require psychotropic medications. These consults are generally telephonic and do not involve the patient. The medical provider is tapping into the clinical expertise of the specialty behavioral health provider to help with managing the patient. Under this model, the primary care or other provider maintains the direct interaction with the patient and prescribes medications based on medical knowledge and input from the consulting psychiatrist.[22]

IMPACT (Improving Mood and Promoting Access to Collaborative Treatment) is a collaborative care model that has been proven to decrease costs of patients even when treated only in primary care. In one study of IMPACT, the return on investment was found to be 6:1, meaning for every $1 dollar spent, $6 were saved. Another study identified significantly reduced pain and depressive symptoms, and improved physical functioning for a group of older adults.[23] Utilizing collaborative care is particularly effective for patients experiencing depression. This evidence-based model has also been recognized as effective in treating chronic pain,[24] anxiety and trauma disorders,[25] and substance use disorders.[26]

Reverse Integration

Reverse integration is when a primary care practitioner provides services in a behavioral health clinic.[27] Within the behavioral health community, providers and advocates believe that individuals diagnosed with serious mental illness or serious emotional disturbances are best served by the existing behavioral health provider, and to have the behavioral health provider take lead responsibility for managing care.[28]

This model has been promoted as a behavioral health home. The Substance Abuse and Mental Health Services Administration (SAMHSA) has advanced the behavioral health home model to integrate care for individuals with mental health and substance use conditions. Certified Community Behavioral Health Clinics (CCBHC) incorporate a philosophy of trauma-informed care. As a CCBHC under SAMHSA grants, the following services must be provided:

- Patient-centered treatment planning
- Primary care screening
- Monitoring of key health indicators and health risk
- Screening, assessment, and diagnosis
- Crisis mental health services
- Outpatient mental health and substance use services
- Targeted case management
- Psychiatric rehabilitation services
- Peer support, counselor services, and family supports
- Intensive, community-based mental healthcare for veterans and members of the armed forces[29]

SAMHSA initially funded programs in the states of Minnesota, Missouri, New Jersey, New York, Oklahoma, Oregon, and Pennsylvania. The funding has expanded to include other states through an expansion grant.[30]

Integrated

With an integrated care model, the behavioral health provider becomes part of the care team and works with the physician and other members of the staff.[31] Generally, the behavioral health clinician does not provide traditional counseling but rather maintains a schedule like a traditional medical practice. The clinician either maintains a separate schedule with 15- to 30-minute appointments or has shared appointments. With shared appointments, the behavioral health clinician joins the physician or other care team member when meeting with patients. This utilizes the behavioral health clinician as a provider extender, like a medical assistant or nurse. The behavioral health clinician is a part of the normal workflow from the perspective of the patient.

The other option in an integrated model is for the physician or other care team member to perform a warm handoff and connect the patient with behavioral health clinician at the end of an office visit.[32] A warm handoff involves making the introduction, explaining the reason why the clinician is present, and smoothly transitioning the visit to the behavioral health clinician before exiting the appointment. One benefit of having an integrated behavior health clinician as part of the care team is that a single, unified care plan is created with defined goals and a standard approach to care. The behavioral health condition is documented in the same EHR system to facilitate communication and retain documentation within one patient record. There is less stigma attached to the appointment due to how the warm handoff or referral is made and the presence of the behavioral health clinician on site.

This approach makes it easier for patients to be transitioned to needed services and fosters an immediate connection with the behavioral health clinician. As part of integrating care, the behavioral health clinician uses shared exam rooms, or has a separate room in the same space. If a separate room is used, maintaining a similar appearance in the room helps ease patient concerns and sets the same tone as being seen for a purely medical reason. In contrast, a traditional treatment room for behavioral health counseling is a quiet room that looks more like a room in a home. Often with a couch and/or comfortable chairs, the space looks nothing like a typical exam room and clinicians often use a white noise machine outside the office to isolate the environment.

Where do I sit? Keeping similar-sized spaces and furnishings minimizes the differences in rooms that are seen by both patients and other team members. However, if family therapy is going to be performed in your practice, it is important to remember to have enough chairs to seat everyone. Also, if traditional group counseling visits are offered, your practice can consider using the waiting room if the sessions are after regular business hours and the space can be dedicated.

When examining the possibility of integrating behavioral healthcare into a medical practice, plan to address barriers. Attitudes about individuals needing mental health or substance use treatment can cause resistance. When the existing team has not been properly educated, these patients may be described as "undesirable people that disrupt the waiting room and disturb other patients" or "junkies shopping for the good stuff." Addressing these biases, whether stated or not, is important to the success of integrating care. If your practice opts to integrate care, use the same techniques outlined in Chapter 3 to implement this new way of providing care. Techniques used with cultural competency (see Chapter 5) are also useful.

Other considerations:

- Changes needed within the EHR and practice management system to support workflows and documentation.

- Billing for integrated care requires new coding and documentation:
  - Some states and payers do not allow same day billing.
  - Billing rules and requirements need to be investigated to determine if billing allows for behavioral services and medical services to be rendered on the same day.
- Licensure requirements.
- Administratively, staff may need additional training around interacting with a patient experiencing poor mental health due to financial issues.

Try creating a cost-benefit analysis of the impact of integrated care on the practice financial results. To complete the analysis, you need to understand current costs while projecting new costs and revenue. Integrated care generates new expenses. There may be a change in productivity for the practice if the physician or other billing team member is able to see more patients per day. For example, if a 15-minute appointment takes less time due to the handoff to address behavioral health concerns, the practice may be able to schedule one or two more appointments per day, increasing the total billable services provided. Or, the integrated care model may alleviate overflow issues when a 15-minute appointment takes closer to 20 or 25 minutes and everyone ends up with a delayed schedule throughout the day.[33, 34, 35]

As you are working through your analysis, gather fee schedules to determine what is reimbursable. Some commercial payers may have a limited set of codes that can be billed. With Medicare and Medicaid, the billable codes may be broader depending on the type of clinician that is hired.

If your analysis indicates that the revenue is not enough to cover the cost of integrated care, you should consider approaching any significant payers with an offer to perform value-based care and be reimbursed using alternative payment models. Approaching a payer with a creative solution may be more welcome than you think.

Some states are offering grants to pilot integrated care or screen for behavior health conditions in addition to federal grants through SAMHSA. However, this funding is usually limited and cannot be relied upon as the funding source to maintain integrated care. Your practice would need to determine how to manage without those funds after the time period of the grant funding. Otherwise the practice may develop much-needed services that are unsustainable. Eliminating services can damage reputation and have other negative consequences.

Resources Outside of Traditional Healthcare

Your practice may also benefit from incorporating resources outside of traditional healthcare. When thinking about the needs of your patients, consider alternatives that support healthy living and appeal to your patients. While some of these resources may not be evidence-based procedures, some patients benefit from alternative and integrative therapies. This is particularly true of patients experiencing pain associated with chronic conditions. Your patients may benefit from your practice integrating alternative care or developing relationships to refer out for services such as:

- Acupuncture
- Acupressure
- Chiropractic manipulation
- Aromatherapy
- Biofeedback
- Neurofeedback
- Massage therapy
- Relaxation therapy,
- General stress reduction
- Yoga

Additionally, patients can benefit from other community resources and linkages. By understanding the general characteristics of the patients seen by your practice, you can tailor your educational information and community resources. Consider factors like age, gender, and commonly diagnosed conditions to narrow down the types of resources that might be most applicable to your patients. Also consider socio-economic factors that influence affordability and accessibility of services. Some resources that may be useful to your patients include:

- Bereavement support
- Lactation consultants
- Childbirth classes
- Community support groups
- Dentistry
- Domestic violence support and shelters
- Faith-based support
- Hospice
- Nutritional counseling
- Parenting classes
- Peer support programs
- Rent and utility assistance
- Respite care
- Transportation

Online listings of local resources can be found at www.auntbertha. com. This is a free resource. Anyone visiting the website can enter a zip code and see a listing of the following service categories:

- Care (child/elder)
- Education
- Housing
- Food
- Goods
- Health

- Money
- Legal
- Transit
- Work

Your practice may be able to find additional resources by visiting your local county or city and state websites for information about public health programs, how to access health insurance, and applying for public assistance. Insurance companies and local hospitals are also resources for information about services and programs available to meet the needs of your patients.

Building the Practice's Situational Awareness

As you continue your practice transformation, you will need to incorporate new services and be aware of resources outside of your practice. Understanding the needs of your patients will help you identify where relationships need to be strengthened within the medical community. Assisting patients to obtain supports to prevent or manage conditions is necessary under value-based care. Connecting patients with resources and services beyond your practice reduces the amount of time that your providers may need to spend with patients to achieve improved outcomes.

CHAPTER 10

Involving the Patient

The healthcare world is full of buzzwords that are tossed around without consistent definition, like "patient-centric," "patient-centered," "patient engagement," "patient experience," "patient activation," and "patient satisfaction."[1] Buzzwords aside, to achieve the Triple Aim, healthcare is required to place the patient at the heart of all activities, with patient preferences and needs shaping individualized care. This will not work unless the patient is actively engaged.

Healthcare providers argue that they are telling patients what to do but that patients are not complying with their directives. This disconnect between providers and patients is due to the largely unrecognized gap in communication and understanding between the physician and patient. Better outcomes occur when a patient is actively engaged in their care, including increases in physical and social health and fewer incidents of depression.

To get patients more involved in their health requires a multi-focal strategy for patient engagement. Most of the focus on patient experience has been about increasing patient satisfaction scores. But the patient experience is about the sum of interactions, relationships, interventions, and resulting outcomes. Patient satisfaction surveys are geared to measure these experiences. These surveys provide quantifiable answers to specific questions associated with the patient experience. They are important sources of information, but they do not measure levels of engagement or patient perceptions. To approach patient engagement, your practice needs to determine your vision of patient engagement and how to best implement that vision. To create that vision, your practice must understand the preferences and needs of its patients to shape the delivery of care.

PERCEPTION OF CARE

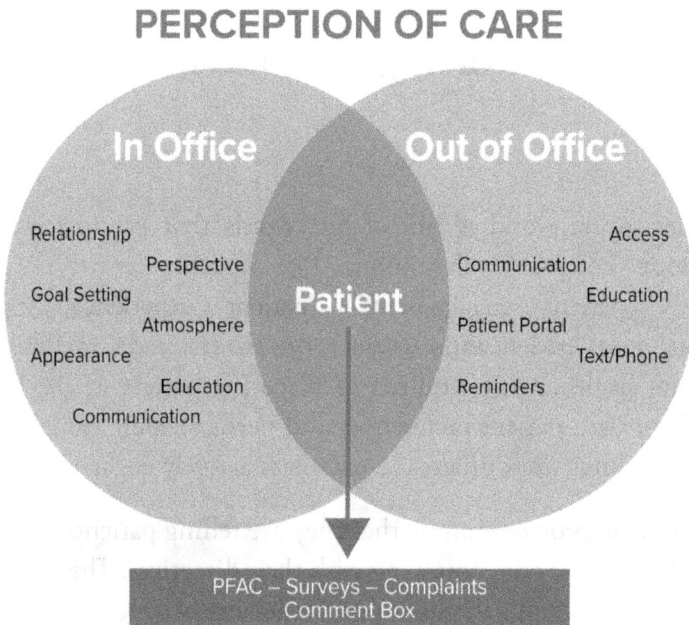

In Office

Relationship
Perspective
Goal Setting
Atmosphere
Appearance
Education
Communication

Out of Office

Access
Communication
Education
Patient Portal
Text/Phone
Reminders

Patient

PFAC – Surveys – Complaints
Comment Box

FIGURE 10.1   Perception of Care

Patient Experience

Each patient has expectations about how care should be delivered, creating a challenge for practices. But in the same way that best practices for medical care are generalized and then tailored to the individual needs of any given patient, your practice can adopt an overall approach to the patient experience that is also individualized.[2] Gathering patient input via different mechanisms (patient satisfaction surveys, grievance forms, suggestions in comment boxes, focus groups, etc.) can be used to create a vision of how healthcare should be delivered.[3] Creating a PFAC (as mentioned in Chapter 2) is another way to gather broad levels of information about the practice and solicit feedback from patients in a deeper, more committed way.[4, 5]

After creating an overarching vision, the specific concrete goals related to outcomes and other metrics of performance are crafted. These overall goals must be filtered to each patient interaction. To accomplish this funneling to a personal level, your practice needs to be aware of how each person wants to engage in his or her healthcare. To ensure appropriate interactions at the individual level, first understand patient engagement.

Patient Engagement

Patient engagement results when a patient is actively involved in their healthcare. This means the patient has the proper knowledge, skills, ability, and willingness to manage their health, under any condition. Getting to this end state is a process that will vary with each person and will continually evolve as health conditions change.

A few different models and theories of patient engagement exist and are all geared to explain how a person becomes activated. Patient

MODELS OF PATIENT ENGAGEMENT

Transtheoretical	Behavioral Economics	Health Belief	Social Cognitive	Patient Health Engagement	Patient Activation
Six stages: • Not ready • Thinking about it • Ready • Taking action • Maintaining	Predictably irrational Immediate loss > long term gain	Triggering event Behavior change is possible Achievable action	Confidence in change Social support	Think-feel-act • Denial • Awareness • Acceptance • Adaptation	Lack understanding Gain knowledge, confidence and skills Action Maintaining

FIGURE 10.2 Models of Patient Engagement

activation is considered a reliable indicator of the ability to self-manage and adhere to treatment.

Transtheoretical model

This model involves the six stages of precontemplation, contemplation, preparation, action, maintenance, and termination. Based on research of individuals at-risk for developing chronic conditions, the group breaks down as roughly 40% in precontemplation, 40% in contemplation and the remaining 20% in preparation.[6] In modifying behaviors, a patient will move through the stages although not at any specified time increment. These six stages can be classified as not ready (precontemplation), getting ready or thinking about it by weighing pros and cons (contemplation), ready or taking action soon (preparation), action or modifying behavior and maintenance where the change is constant and becomes a part of routine life.

Behavioral economics

This model is based on the premise that patients and physicians are viewed as "predictably irrational" and will not make the best choices. Further, that people are more sensitive to the idea of suffering a loss than the possibility of gaining a benefit. In trying to adopt new behaviors, a patient relates closely to the immediate loss of the behavior that must change along with whatever emotional components that the behavior satisfies. For example, a patient visualizes the short-term loss of enjoying dessert more readily that the long-term gain of weighing less and not taking insulin to control diabetes. The patient cannot see the long-term gains (health) over the short-term loss (no dessert). To activate change, the patient needs to perceive an immediate loss that is greater than a loss of changing the behavior.

This model may be harder to implement within your practice because of the inability to create that type of loss. Some employers are deploying this model by creating an incentive for the behavior change through offering rewards for activities like documenting exercise or joining a gym, while extracting financial penalties for unhealthy behaviors like smoking. In this case, the loss of time associated with exercise is less than the financial loss for continuing to smoke. To use this model, a patient would need to identify offsetting gains and losses to overcome the lack of activation.

Health belief model

In this model a person believes that changing behavior will avoid sickness, or if already ill, allow for healing. The individual will then take specific action to either prevent the illness or reverse the sickness. Patient activation is influenced by how the patient perceives the likelihood of being susceptible, the severity or consequences of the illness, and the pros and cons of acting. For this model to be effective, the patient may need to experience a triggering event personally or be exposed to someone else's experience. An example is having a heart attack or a family member having a heart attack, triggering behavior change. Lastly, the model considers whether the patient believes that actions can be accomplished, and behavior change is possible.

Social cognitive theory

This model is based on the theory that behavior is influenced by whether or not a person believes she or he has the ability to change. This confidence in being able to change is influenced by past success or failure in attempting to change and whether the person's social community supports change. To encourage the patient to change behaviors, a provider focuses on building the patient's confidence about the ability to improve their health and offers support in the process.

Patient health engagement model (PHE model)

In this model a patient moves through four stages that consider how the patient thinks, feels, and acts.

- First stage
  - The patient is in a state of blackout or disengagement, feeling overwhelmed and not aware or not knowing how to react to a diagnosis.
- Second stage
  - The patient recognizes that "I am an ill body" and is hypersensitive to symptoms but has limited knowledge and ability to self-manage.
- Third stage
  - The patient has accepted the condition, and has some knowledge and skills to be compliant, but is not ready to fully self-manage. At this stage, the person realizes that the condition is a part of who they are but not what defines them as a person.
- Fourth stage
  - The patient has the skills and knowledge to manage the condition, has overcome any psychological trauma related to the disease onset, and can adapt to ever-changing circumstances.

Patient activation model® (PAM®):

Under this model a patient moves through levels of activation where they understand the need for taking a role in his or her healthcare, has the confidence and knowledge to manage it, takes action, and stays the course.

- Level 1
  - The patient is just starting to understand the need to take a role in his or her own health but is likely to be passive.
- Level 2
  - The patient is building knowledge and confidence but is still lacking in basic information.
- Level 3
  - The patient is taking action but may not have the full confidence and skills to manage the condition.

- Level 4
  - ○ The patient is maintaining new behaviors but may have difficulty during times of crisis or stress.

Several measures are available to assess patients. Among them, these four examples have been validated.

- The English and Spanish Self-Efficacy to Manage Chronic Disease Scale (SEMCD and SEMCD-S)[7, 8]
- the How's Your Health patient survey, validated for low-literacy patients[9]
- the PHE Scale: Measuring Patient Engagement, and[10, 11]
- the Patient Activation Measure (PAM)®.[12]

These specific tools are documents to be completed by the patient. Each measure has different strengths and weaknesses and assists with understanding the patient's level of engagement. You may find that understanding different models and theories may offer a better perspective of patient activation and engagement even if a specific tool is not administered.

Whichever measure is selected to gain insight into patient engagement, ensuring that the care team and members of the office understand the importance of patient engagement is critical to successfully change the culture and delivery of care within your practice. Take the time to train staff and explain how improving patient engagement and the patient experience results in better health outcomes. As described in the team development section of Chapter 8, staff need to understand their roles and responsibilities in patient engagement. Workflows, policies, and procedures should support and encourage patient engagement. Evaluating the commitment of your staff to patient engagement can be part of the annual review process. However, there should also be rewards and recognition during the implementation and startup of this new way of delivering care. Creating positive incentives that are fun and encouraging staff along the way can be helpful.

In-Office Approach to Patient Involvement

During interactions with patients, your staff and providers should keep in mind the convergence of factors that affect patient activation and engagement. Planning for how you encourage patient activation helps you prepare for patient interactions. These interactions occur between communication, education, coaching, online health information—which contributes to or detracts from the patient's knowledge, and patient skills, ability, confidence, and willingness to change.

Factors that impact the patient's ability to manage their own healthcare are:

- Health literacy
- Education level
- Confidence in being able to manage their health
- Level of familial and community support
- Social determinants of health
- Mental readiness/willingness
- Knowledge about their condition
- Life experience

All these factors interact with one another. Staff and providers should consider the impacts they have on their patients. Patient engagement begins the first time they walk through the doors. The way the patients are treated and what they experience from that moment on colors their perceptions and impacts their potential for engagement. This initial interaction sets the tone and expectations for the patient. Despite a positive relationship with the provider, difficulties in interactions with the rest of the team affects the likelihood of patient engagement, following directions, and even whether the patient chooses to continue care with that particular practice.

Impact of life experience: As an example, if you are conveying to a person the importance of oral health, the patient may not comprehend the idea of keeping healthy teeth, because everyone around them has lost their teeth and oral hygiene is not common. The person views losing teeth as normal and inevitable.

The caregiver-patient relationship can sometimes be a critical factor to a patient's health and wellness, particularly with children and older adults. While the focus should be on the patient, involving the caregiver and being aware of their concerns can assist the patient in complying with directions and shared goals. As an example, if a pediatric patient needs to change nutritional habits, the parent or caregiver must understand proper nutrition that is based on the child's specific needs. With an older patient, there may be a need for the caregiver to offer more support and have greater availability. If the caregiver is an adult child of the patient, there may be issues with the amount of time that the caregiver has available. The care team may need to assess the caregiver's level of knowledge, skills, ability, and willingness. This does not mean the provider or care team gets involved in family issues. But to achieve better outcomes, the role of the caregiver cannot be overlooked.

Whatever can be done to strengthen the patient's relationship with the practice staff and providers will improve the level of patient engagement. A trusted relationship is one of the hallmarks of good patient care. Physicians, nurses, and other healthcare providers understand the importance of having a good working relationship with patients, particularly those with chronic conditions. Developing trust as part of that relationship is the goal. Trust makes the patient more willing to listen to what the provider has to say and increases the likelihood the patient will engage in change.

Communication

A communication gap between patients and care team members will inhibit patient engagement.[13] Communications should use plain language and be geared toward the literacy level of the patient. If literacy levels are unknown, a good rule of thumb is to gear communications to a sixth-grade level. This includes both written and verbal communication. When a provider is communicating with the patient, the goal is to remember the acronym KISS: Keep It Simple and Specific.[14] Let a literacy assessment (as mentioned above) guide the team in understanding what "simple" means for each patient.

Communication would not be specific, for instance, if a patient were told to "eat better." Take a situation where the patient needs to reduce cholesterol or fat intake. Even saying to reduce cholesterol and fat intake may not be specific enough. Being direct about consuming more vegetables, poultry, and lean meats, while limiting dairy and bread, is more specific. What "healthy eating" means must be defined for that patient. Patient engagement will be impacted by how sensitive topics like unhealthy behaviors are handled. If care is not taken, patients may feel judged and become defensive. These feelings will alienate the patient from the team's communications and cause them to lose trust in their providers. Additionally, care must be taken when relaying information about chronic and life-changing conditions. Supportive conversations help patients engage more successfully in their own health.

Education

Backing up information with written educational documents and access to supporting materials either online or through a portal helps ensure retention of information. Also, important to remember is that often information needs to be conveyed more than one time to a patient to ensure comprehension. Rarely is information fully absorbed after an initial discussion. The level of information patients need also changes as management of their condition changes. Information to convey to patients beyond managing conditions are things like knowing when to report safety concerns or near misses, particularly with medications. A patient should understand when changes in health can be handled by calling the office or if the incident requires seeking additional help. When patients fully comprehend this type of information, unnecessary complications and inappropriate emergency department usage is avoided.

For patients to be able to manage their own health and wellness, education and coaching may be needed. Statistics from the National Assessment of Adult Literacy indicate that only 12% of Americans have proficient health literacy.[15] Given this level of literacy, assessing what patients understand about care goals and medical instructions is critical. Tools for assessing health literacy (i.e., REALM-SF, SAHL-E, and SAHL-S) are available online.[16, 17] Another good resource is the AHRQ Health Literacy Universal Precautions Toolkit.[18]

Goal Setting

When setting goals for a patient as part of care planning, the identified goals should be specific and achievable. Important to remember is that achievable is defined by the patient not by the care team. Developing goals requires input from the patient. By setting goals that allow the patient to see progress in small steps, the patient is encouraged and confidence in the ability to change is reinforced. Be sure to use goals that have specific timelines to create accountability.

Care planning discussions require open-ended questions and encouragement for patients to speak up about any concerns. To facilitate the discussion, providers can use techniques like motivational interviewing. The care team should be educated on how to use motivational interviewing before attempting to use this technique with patients. The elements of motivational interviewing are:

- Encourage the patient to discuss the need for change and reasons he or she has for wanting to change.

- Use reflective listening to understand the patients' perspectives about the need to, and reasons for change; reiterate what is heard to confirm that patients are understood.
- Express empathy and obtain a commitment to change.
- Identify how patients' current behaviors differ from the stated goals.
- Avoid confrontation and arguing with patients.
- Work to change patient resistance and avoid direct opposition.
- Encourage and support the patients' beliefs in their ability to succeed.

Motivational interviewing helps to identify goals and encourages the patient to commit to change. However, consideration needs to be given to each patient's level of activation. Setting goals is more difficult when patients are not ready to take ownership of, or participate in, their health.

Another way to facilitate discussion and create shared goals is to use shared decision-making aids.[19] The purpose of shared decision-making aids is to provide information to patients to allow for informed decisions. With shared decision-making, patients:

- gain additional information about general health and specific health conditions,
- are informed about decisions that need to be made, and
- understand the pros and cons of options.

When patients are involved in shared decision-making, the level of activation is increased, with the patient more likely to follow through with the decision.[20] When reviewing information with patients, listening to their preferences and helping them understand available options is an essential part of the process. These tools are particularly useful when going over options for medication.

An example of a shared decision-making tool is a document produced by the Mayo Clinic to assist diabetes patients with the decision of whether to take statins.[21] The aid communicates in simple written language as well as pictures showing color-coded smiley faces. The three parts of the aid walk the patient through the statistical likelihood of certain consequences of taking statins as well as some of the negative effects. The final section includes a question that allows the patient the option to take statins, not take statins, or to decide at some other time.

Another example of a shared decision-making aid is one that describes antidepressants used to treat depression.[22] The aid shows several different classes of antidepressants, including SSRIs, SNRIs, and TCAs along with a scale that shows the likelihood of weight loss or weight gain. On a similar type of scale, the guide also describes how the same medications can affect sexual issues and sleep, and if stopping the medication will make the patient feel ill. The information presents key factors to consider when deciding about medications, including cost. The tool offers a framework for a conversation to discuss medication options and potential side effects that places the patient in control.

As can be seen from these two examples of shared decision-making aids, the patient is provided information to allow for an informed decision, even if that decision is to not decide. This information can be documented in the patient records and then be revisited at a future date. Aids for shared decision-making are available for a variety of topics and often at no charge.[23, 24]

Changing Your Perspective

The relationship with the provider is influenced by many different components, including the provider's perception of the patient. Perceptions can be based on cultural factors, preconceived notions or stereotypes, and unconscious bias. Another factor influencing the relationship with a patient is the level of communication between the doctor or team and the patient. How patients are treated and the attitude and delivery of customer service within the office also influences engagement. With the relationship being a key aspect of patient engagement, fostering a relationship between patient and moving to care teams further solidifies that relationship with your practice.

As your level of awareness increases, you may start to realize that your perspective changes about interactions with patients. This may include perceptions about people that have been labeled in the past as "problem" patients. Take the time to think about all the factors that influence a patient including their skills, knowledge, confidence, and willingness to change.

> **I read on the internet that ...** While discussing information patients find online may be annoying, see them as people engaged in understanding their health options. By restructuring this conversation, you may be able to direct the patient to better understand the condition or topic and also identify sources of information that are more reliable.

Out of Office Approach to Patient Involvement

The amount of time that a provider spends directly interacting with the patient is very limited. To help support a patient outside of face-to-face visits, your practice can offer additional support using technology and other outreach methods.

Patient Portal

A patient portal can be a useful patient engagement tool if a person has online access and understands what is in the portal.[25] Currently, most portals allow for two-way messaging, requesting appointments, medication refills, and high-level information like the after-visit summaries.[26] The ability to exchange secure messages offers patients flexibility and can eliminate unnecessary visits. With access to the portal when convenient for them, your patients can make requests at any time of the day without being overheard. Portals offer the ability to send written communication in a way that mirrors the 24/7 connectivity experienced in daily life.

Some portals are configured to allow the patient to access detailed information like lab test results or, for children, growth charts. Communication within the portal may also include reminders about upcoming appointments and alerts for patients regarding educational campaigns like a reminder to be vaccinated against the flu. The portal offers many benefits to the patient and can reduce the number of calls to the practice. Portals provide practices with many opportunities to communicate with their patients.

One of the issues with patient portals is that a patient with multiple providers could have multiple portals. Without a level of coordination, a patient could easily get overwhelmed and confused. Current regulatory standards are pushing toward interoperability of health information, which would help mitigate this issue.[27] With full interoperability, every provider involved in a patient's care could have direct access to the patient's record. This would help mitigate issues where patients cannot recall all information provided, tests given, test results, care provided, and medications prescribed. Given the current track record of electronic health records and resistance to data sharing, much will have to change within the industry to achieve interoperability.

Other Technology

Many provider offices have adopted the use of either texting and/or automated calls, primarily for appointment reminders. With patient permission, the use of texting can be expanded to provide a reminder to take medications or other aspects of the prescribed care plan.

As part of the planning process, and tied to population health initiatives, your practice can establish an overall calendar for educational outreach. Using a pediatric practice as an example, the calendars can include creating reminders to schedule physicals in April and May and flu vaccines in September and October. The prepared calendar identifies when the texts or other communications are to be sent.

Many mobile apps for both providers and patients are available. Depending on the EHR system the practice uses or the condition a patient is managing, the practice should investigate available resources and be prepared to assess and integrate them into their communication plans and processes. Younger patients might appreciate their providers engaging them with technology that meets them "where they are at."

Patient Satisfaction

Currently, patient satisfaction is a subject of much discussion and often used as an indicator of the patient experience. In 2006, a patient satisfaction survey (HCAHPS) was required of hospitals. In 2008, the results of the surveys were made public. Hospitals now have payments tied to levels of patient satisfaction equally weighted with care coordination and other clinical activities. This has sharply increased the focus on patient satisfaction. What most people think of as patient satisfaction are the survey results scores from HCAHPS or CG-CAHPS. The surveys are tools to measure satisfaction and the score is influenced by many different aspects of patient interactions. These aspects include patient care as well as the patient's perception of their overall health, including their experiences with providers and the healthcare team.

Healthgrades is an online forum where information is posted about individual healthcare providers. On this forum, people post comments and reviews, as well as rate a provider. According to the Healthgrades website, this feedback collected is based on nine questions adapted from the CG-CAHPS survey.[28] Reviews and comments were analyzed from information posted on Healthgrades. Satisfaction and comments were noted to be mostly about perceptions and feelings, not outcomes and specific clinical results.

The outcome of a study prepared by Healthgrades and MGMA revealed that nonclinical factors are the most important criteria in the overall patient experience. These factors include the personality of and interactions with the physician and other members of the office staff, as well as the amount of time spent with the physician.[29] Understanding this general trend in patient experience reinforces the importance of communication and interaction. Patient experience encompasses the sum of all interactions with your practice, whether face-to-face or through technology.

Improving patients' experiences depends upon them feeling valued and respected in all interactions. A practice's staff being willing to stop and listen to a patient can make the difference between engagement and looking for a new practice. Word-of-mouth and online ratings matter. Many patients will consult online reviews and read the practice website before selecting a provider. Read the online reviews and assess your own patient surveys for areas where the practice may not be delivering on patient expectations.

When starting to evaluate the patient experience, examine the touch points where patient interacts with the practice. Adopting an understanding that without the patient there is no reason for the practice to exist, your practice can shift to be more patient-centered and deliver high value customer service. The patient experience starts with the first call. Although the front desk person may not be actively involved as part of the clinical care team, he or she represents the office and is a part of the overall care and office team. Being able to express empathy and friendliness results in a more positive patient experience.

When the patient arrives, the appearance and general atmosphere of the office also creates impressions. If there is a sense of chaos or stress, the patient will pick up on it. The office environment should promote a sense of calm and safety. The layout and design of your waiting room can help promote a sense of comfort. This applies not only to the comfort and arrangement of the chairs but also to what is available to the patient in the waiting room. Reviewing patients that are scheduled for new patient visits or well checks is a simple way to identify those that can be extended a special touch.

> **Where's the charger?** Another cost effective, friendly touch is to provide a charging station for electronic devices in the waiting room. Many people opt to use a smart phone to keep occupied rather than reading a magazine.

The space in the waiting room can also be a great place to encourage patient education. Offering written materials with relevant topics and displaying posters or other wall hangings communicates educational information. Consider playing educational material on a TV or computer screen. These educational materials can be purchased from independent third parties. Or better yet, your practice could create recordings of your physicians and staff talking about the practice, your approach to care, and the importance of your patients. Creating these types of videos can be done using everyday technology like an iPhone, but if your practice can afford to do so, hire a professional videographer for a more polished looking result. Information in the waiting room about community resources that meet the needs of the patient population is also helpful.

Developing the Relationship with the Patient

The patient experience is about more than clinical outcomes and effectiveness of care. The patient experience includes how the patient perceives being treated. One of the negative outcomes of the computerized patient records is that healthcare has become checklist-oriented and task-driven. Engaging patients requires putting them in the center of their care and encouraging active participation. While the term customer service tends to have a negative context in healthcare, healthcare must be about the patient. This means structuring your practice to make the patient feel appreciated, valued, and respected.

By developing a relationship with each patient, your practice can ensure that the patient continues to receive treatment with your practice and have a higher likelihood of achieving better health outcomes. Your approach to the delivery of care and focus on a patient-centered approach can differentiate your practice, generate positive reviews, and spread word of mouth referrals to patients and other providers or facilities in the local healthcare system. What your patients say about your practice or organization should be compared to the mission and values you wish to promote.

Chapter 11

Getting Reimbursed

The goal and challenge of value-based care is to marry financial, clinical, and quality outcomes. When managed care was first introduced, the focus was primarily on utilization, which often restricted care. While this lowered costs, quality suffered. Having a healthcare system that pays for services based on volume with no connection to quality has also failed. The new paradigm utilizes APMs, which are grounded in the principles of value-based care.

To successfully transform your practice to value-based care, financial resources must be identified that enable the practice to transition to demonstrating outcomes that qualify for value-based payments. The financial pressure during the transition period can be one of the biggest challenges your practice will face. In some cases, a dip in financial results occurs from spending money to gain future benefit. However, this cost to transform must be balanced against the cost of not transforming and the potential lost future revenue. The uncertainty when projecting new revenues and costs can be challenging to accept and overcome. Assessments about the likelihood of value-based payments continuing to expand also generates resistance. Generating the needed funding can come from approaching payers with a proposal that supports the transition to value-based care.

Research Your Options

In researching available funding, the best place to start is with your major payers. In both Medicaid and Medicare markets, the government is contractually requiring the use of value-based payment programs. In managed Medicaid contracts, CMS is requiring states to adopt standardized models to promote consistency among payers and to have specific percentages of provider payments in value-based payment programs.

It varies by state, but generally the percentage of care in value-based payments is required to increase every year. Initially, health plans may meet the requirements by contracting for value-based payments using lower levels of payments types like pay for reporting of quality measures.[1] But over time, health plans need to contract using more sophisticated payment methodologies as defined in the spectrum of APMs.[2] To avoid penalties, health plans will be looking to increase participation in value-based payments. In New York, the goal is to have 80% of all payments be value-based by 2021. As of 2016, less than 25% of the market participate in APMs.

Health plans and insurers in the commercial space are also looking to encourage adoption of value-based care. Payers continue to create new value-based programs.[3] Given the requirements to move to value-based care, practices have leverage in approaching the payer with a business case that requests funding to support the practice transformation. The payer will evaluate the projected care savings, incentive earnings, and penalties associated with their contractual requirements against the cost to help support provider transformation. Practices that do not move forward with value-based payments could face a situation where their services no longer meet provider network adequacy and/or the health plan begins to mandate contractual value-based payments. When this happens, your practice may face being removed from the network or being too late to receive assistance from payers to transform your practice to support the delivery of value-based care.

As demonstrated in the infographic below, payers overwhelmingly believe APM activity will increase. They are reporting that the barriers are on the provider side, and that health plans are interested in APMs and ready to implement APM programs.

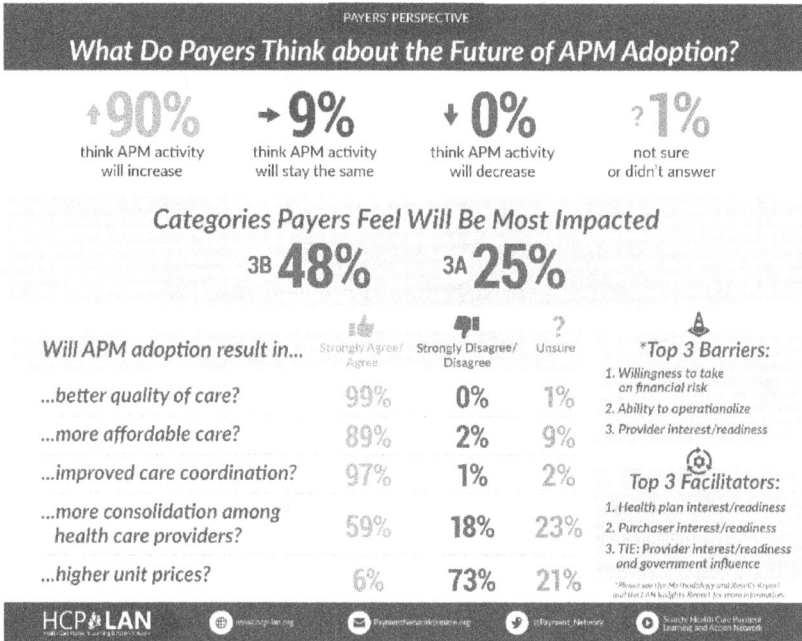

FIGURE 11.1 Payers' Perspective Infographic

Source: *Healthcare Payment Learning & Action Network. Measuring Progress: Adoption of Alternative Payment Models in Commercial, Medicaid, Medicare Advantage, and Fee-for-Service Medicare Programs. Released October 22, 2018.*

Value-Based Payment Financing Models

To encourage adoption of a value-based care approach, the reimbursement within healthcare is changing to APMs. An APM connects value and quality to payment rather than just paying for a service to be rendered. As mentioned in Chapter 1, HHS created the LAN through CMS. In 2017, the LAN, in conjunction with the CMS Alliance to Modernize Healthcare (CAMH), finalized the APM Framework, a methodology to be used to track progress toward payment reform. The eight principles of the APM Framework are summarized as follows:

- Changing providers' financial incentives is not sufficient to achieve person-centered care, so it will be essential to empower patients to be partners in health care transformation.

- Reformed payment mechanisms will only be as successful as the delivery system capabilities and innovations they support.

- The goal for payment reform is to transition health care payments from FFS to APMs. While Category 2C APMs can be the payment model for some providers, most national spending should continue moving into Categories 3 and 4.

- Value-based incentives should ideally reach care teams who deliver care.

- Payment models that do not take quality into account are not considered APMs in the APM Framework, and do not count as progress toward payment reform.

- Value-based incentives should be intense enough to motivate providers to invest in and adopt new approaches to care delivery, without subjecting providers to financial and clinical risk they cannot manage.

- APMs will be classified according to the dominant form of payment when using more than one type of payment.

- Centers of excellence, accountable care organizations, and patient-centered medical homes are examples, rather than Categories, in the APM Framework because they are delivery systems that can be applied to and supported by a variety of payment models.[4]

The APM Framework

The APM Framework has four categories and eight subcategories, which are shown below.

APM FRAMEWORK

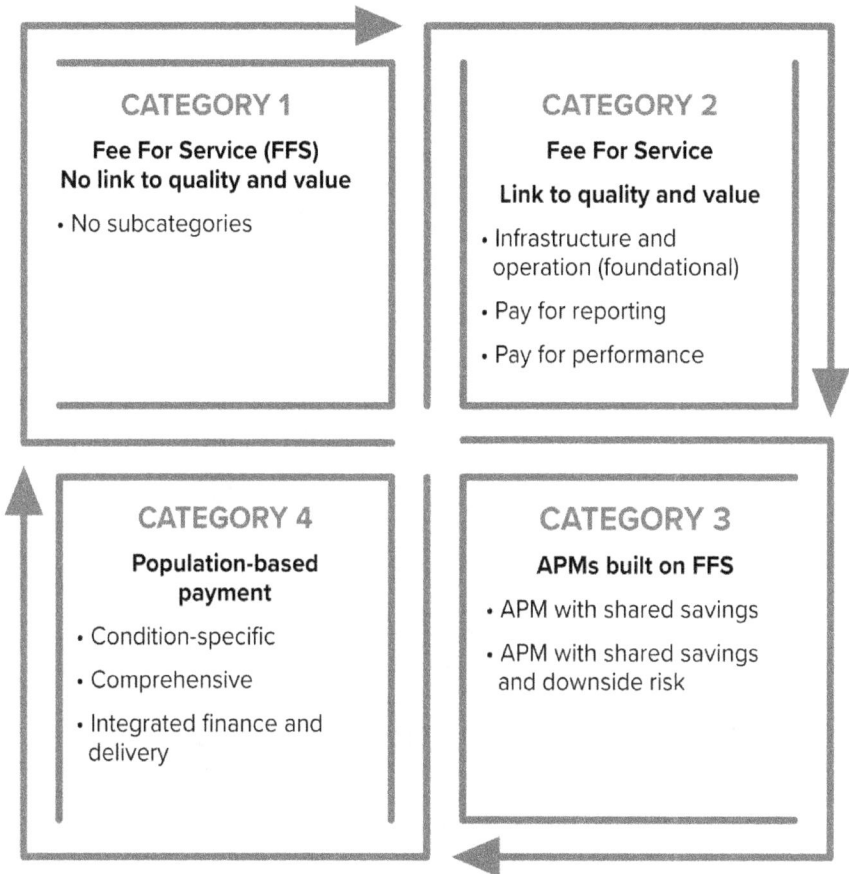

CATEGORY 1

Fee For Service (FFS)
No link to quality and value

- No subcategories

CATEGORY 2

Fee For Service

Link to quality and value

- Infrastructure and operation (foundational)
- Pay for reporting
- Pay for performance

CATEGORY 4

Population-based payment

- Condition-specific
- Comprehensive
- Integrated finance and delivery

CATEGORY 3

APMs built on FFS

- APM with shared savings
- APM with shared savings and downside risk

FIGURE 11.2   APM Framework

Source: *Healthcare Payment Learning & Action Network. Measuring Progress: Adoption of Alternative Payment Models in Commercial, Medicaid, Medicare Advantage, and Fee-for-Service Medicare Programs. Released October 22, 2018.*

Based on a study released October 22, 2018, the most healthcare dollars remain in Category 1 with payments that are not tied to quality.[5, 6] The spending below represents an increase in Category 2 payments where FFS reimbursement is linked to quality and value and an increase in

Categories 3 and 4. The following depicts the results of the surveys from the last three years:

ADOPTION OF APMs

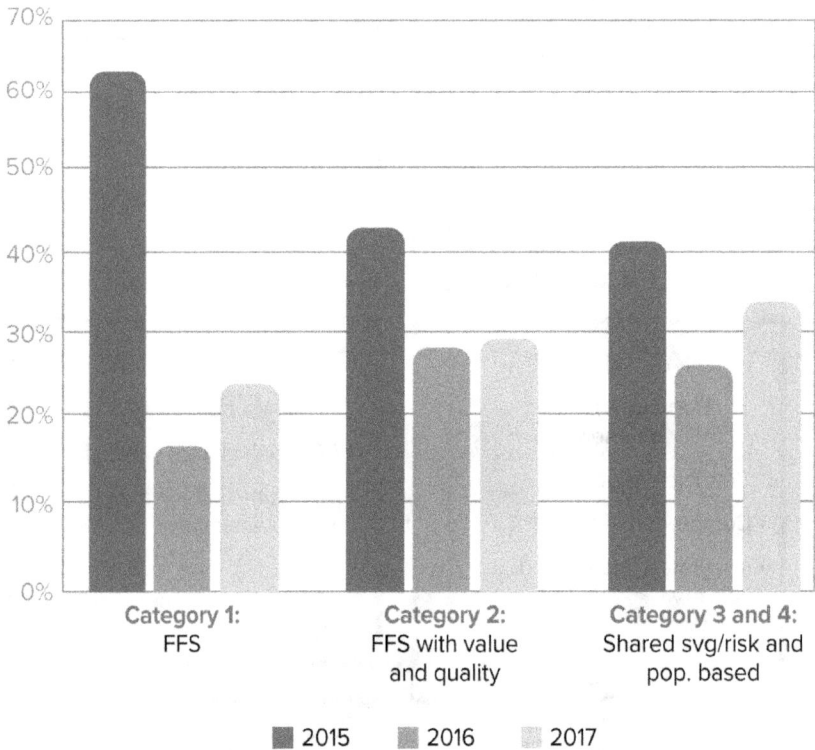

FIGURE 11.3   Adoption of APMs

Source: *Healthcare Payment Learning & Action Network. Measuring Progress: Adoption of Alternative Payment Models in Commercial, Medicaid, Medicare Advantage, and Fee-for-Service Medicare Programs. Released October 22, 2018.*

Understanding Financial Basics

In evaluating the move to value-based care, both the costs and benefits need to be evaluated. As mentioned in Chapter 2, developing a traditional CBA or ROI analysis is your starting point for evaluating the financial component of a transition. With the CBA, you examine the total costs related to the total benefits. Depending on your financial objectives, the goal is generally to have the benefits be greater than the costs to move forward with a project. In assessing the ROI, the net benefit is divided by the total cost and multiplied by 100, expressing a percentage. The higher the percentage, the greater the ROI.

> For some organizations, a specific ROI must be achieved in order for a project to be funded. For others, it is just a metric to help set milestones and make decisions. The need to achieve a certain ROI can create a budget cap for expenses or help practices focus on maximizing revenues and benefits. **Leadership must help determine how you use your ROI metric.**

Both cost-benefit and ROI analyses require the development of costs and benefits. Note that benefits may include more than just the amount of actual revenue. Intangible benefits like increasing position in the marketplace or creating barriers for competitors are benefits as well. Another aspect to consider is whether you are meeting a minimum regulatory mandate or network requirement. Determining these is often difficult but their values should be considered in any analysis.

Quantifying expenses is an easier starting point than projecting revenues. The expenses are then compared to projected revenues to determine whether costs are higher or lower than the total anticipated revenue. If you find that costs exceed revenue, evaluate if expenses can be reduced, revenue increased (through further negotiations or identifying new funding sources), or if the project should be suspended.

Determining Costs

The first step in financially assessing the move to value-based care is to calculate the cost of transformation. When evaluating how your practice currently operates compared to what is needed to deliver outcomes, start with developing a gap analysis. The gap analysis identifies actions to take and cost elements. From there, translate the findings into a project plan that identifies all the actions that need to be taken to change operations to the desired result.

In the project plan, you can not only identify the people and technology resources but also estimate the projected cost to complete the task, thus creating a project budget. In the same plan you should also identify the timing of when actions need to be started and completed. From a financial perspective, the pace of activity makes a difference. Some costs will be incurred sooner than others. This will affect the need for cash flow or cash resources to pay for completion of tasks. If your project plan lasts longer than 6 to 12 months, your finance person can project those additional costs into a future budget period.

When considering expenses, the following general categories can be used to quantify cost:

- Personnel
  - payroll and benefits for all staff
- Incentives
  - additional provider or team compensation or bonuses
- Facilities
  - office rent or mortgage payments, utilities, and related maintenance services like janitorial
- Professional services
  - consulting and other contracted services in place of personnel
- Patient education
  - such as office supplies or printing and mailing costs related to outreach or educational materials
- Professional dues and subscriptions
  - fees charged for associations and trade journals
- Inventory and medical supplies
  - materials used in the delivery of care

- Insurance
  - all coverage types including malpractice, general liability, etc.
- Training and meetings
  - internal and external training or conferences as well as meeting cost for things like providing beverages and food
- Travel
  - mileage for local commutes, non-local transportation, and lodging
- Equipment and IT
  - software and hardware, including costs related to reporting, data management, and electronic health records
- Other
  - general category to capture anything not classified elsewhere

To make the analysis as meaningful as possible, this list should be modified to reflect how your practice operates. In developing costs, estimate the incremental cost associated with each task or major task grouping. An example of an incremental cost is if you were to purchase a specific module for your EHR that you would not have otherwise purchased. The cost of that module would be incorporated into your expenses associated with the transformation project. If the module is only partially related to the transition, use your best judgment to estimate the percentage associated with the project to avoid overloading expenses that are not directly attributable to changing how your practice operates.

When developing this analysis, the cost to see a patient needs to be determined. To calculate the average cost of a patient visit, determine the total expenses for a period as well as the total number of services delivered. In general, the cost can be calculated by taking the total expense divided by the number of visits. However, consider the differences in the types of billing codes used on each visit. Using relative value units (RVUs) or some other measure can help mitigate the differences in the levels of effort to deliver one service versus another service.[7, 8] An example of this difference is illustrated by looking at a 15-minute visit versus a 30-minute visit, or the complexity as defined by the billed evaluation and management (E&M) code. To simplify the illustration, the following example uses a weighted-average—and assumes the base for determining differences is time. The base unit is defined as 15 minutes.

> **Calculating average cost of a patient visit:** Assume that there are 26 patients seen per day, and 20 are for 15-minute visits and 6 are for 30-minute visits. In a month with 20 working days, the total number of patients seen is 572. By assigning a value based on 15-minute increments, the 15-minute visit is assigned a value of 1 and the 30-minute visit is assigned a value of 2 (30 minutes divided by 15 minutes is 2). Assuming a total monthly cost of $52,500, the cost to deliver 15 minutes of care is $74.57, making the cost of a 15-minute visit $74.57, and $149.15 for a 30-minute visit.

TABLE 11.1   Calculating Average Cost of a Patient Visit

	15 min	30 min	Total
Patients/day	20	6	26
Days/month	22	22	22
Value of base units	1	2	1.23
Total base units	440	264	704
Total costs			$52,500
Cost per unit based on value	$74.57	$149.15	

By completing this level of analysis, you can identify the cost to deliver care based on the existing reimbursement structures. This approach is a simplified example. More advanced cost analysis can be completed to further refine the costs. Generally, a more advanced approach involves categorizing the direct, indirect, and overhead costs. Allocating the expenses to specific services requires identifying the appropriate basis for apportioning indirect and overhead costs to direct expenses. This analysis can further define expenses by clinic or other significant characteristics like payer, office location, and treating physician or care team. Understanding your costs will impact your ability to evaluate options under value-based payment programs and negotiate from a strong position with payers.

Projecting Revenue

Expenses are one side of the equation and the other is revenue. Currently, revenue is primarily based on the number of services delivered and the type or complexity of the service as defined by the billing code. Reimbursement varies based on the specific amounts negotiated with each payer. Also affecting revenue are write-offs of bad debt and uncollectible costs like self-pay patients, co-pays, or denials. In the current FFS system, estimated revenue can generally be based on past trends in the total volume of services delivered by each provider adjusted by the mix of insurance reimbursement levels. With value-based payment programs, you need to consider not only the reimbursement on a per-service basis but also incentives if you are participating at lower levels within the APM Framework. The analysis for APM Category 2 payments is the most straightforward: reimbursement is FFS-based with additional payments related to quality. As the complexity of the payments increases, as it does for APM Categories 3 and 4, costs must be projected for different payment types, such as case rates, bundled payments, or capitation.

Additional sources of revenue to consider in your CBA are incentive payments, supplemental/higher reimbursements for existing services, and reimbursement for new services. To project the increased revenue associated with providing a new service, estimate the total number of visits associated with the higher reimbursement for new services. For example, if your practice is going to conduct depression screenings, estimate the number of patients to be screened and multiply that times the reimbursement for the screening (50 patients/month x $2 per screening x 12 months = $1,200 per year). If your practice negotiates a higher reimbursement for a service already being delivered, estimate the number of services times the difference between the higher reimbursement and the current reimbursement. As an example, assume that you are being paid $10 more per office visit if you report three quality measures. If the current reimbursement is $50 a visit, the new reimbursement is $60 dollars a visit and you see 200 patients a month, your calculation would be ($60-$50 or $10) x 200 patients x12 months = $24,000 per year.

When considering the type of APM that your practice is interested in pursuing, keep in mind that the level of financial risk differs based on the payment mechanism. FFS has the least amount of risk because your practice is paid for each service delivered. Most providers have already determined how to generate profits by comparing their FFS revenue to their cost to perform the service. The following diagram depicts types of reimbursement and indicates an increasing level of financial risk:

LEVEL OF FINANCIAL RISK

FIGURE 11.4 Level of Financial Risk

The forms of payment can include:

- FFS
    - ○ The provider is paid for services delivered without any quality measures.

- Performance-based FFS
  - The provider receives payment for each service delivered but includes additional payment for reporting, performance, and/or infrastructure and operations.
- Shared savings
  - The provider payment includes a mechanism to share in savings from cost reductions, the provider shares only in the upside and has no risk for losses.
- Shared risk
  - Payment includes a mechanism for sharing in savings and losses, generally this is tied to a risk corridor where care costs have an established target and differences to that target are shared between the provider and the insurer.
- Capitation with performance-based measures
  - The provider bears all the risks and rewards based on a set amount paid to the provider, usually on a per-member per-month basis and must meet established performance metrics.

The best form of alternative payments for your organization will depend upon your infrastructure, risk tolerance, and ability to manage operational and financial targets. You also need to ensure that you have executive buy-in and support. The higher the level of financial risk, the greater the need for clinical integration and the ability to manage data to monitor and track performance against established targets.

Making the Business Case

When moving into value-based payments, your organization or practice should adopt the attitude of "better to learn to walk before you run." If you have no experience in managing financial risk, start with value-based payments that are a Category 2 APM, where you are reimbursed on an FFS basis with incentives.

Another option is to consider a case rate that does not require clinical integration (unless your practice includes a variety of specialties or has some level of integration where being responsible for an episode of care makes sense). For some practices, case rates have been in place for a long period of time.

> **Example:** Maternity case rates are common, at least for the physician component. A broader maternity case rate could include not only prenatal and postnatal visits but also the facility component for the inpatient admission. The case rate could also include responsibility for any readmissions or other follow-up care associated with the pregnancy and delivery.

Risk with case rates is minimized when the services involved in the case rate are well-known, easy to project, and have little variation.

As you work to build a business case for moving into value-based care, consider the audiences to whom you are directing the business case to convince that this is the right direction for your practice. This audience could include both leadership and your major payers, which requires slightly different approaches. The business case to your leadership should be structured to address any concerns that may arise internally and will be specific to your circumstances. The central question to be answered, regardless of the intended audience, is why the transition to value-based care be should funded over all other competing priorities. Your business case needs to clearly articulate the answer to this core question. Think of answering "what's in it for me" for your audience.

Know What Motivates a Payer

Before approaching a payer with a business proposal to move to value-based care, research how the payer is positioned in the market, its contractual requirements for government business, and its current performance (particularly around HEDIS measures). HEDIS is the abbreviation for the Healthcare Effectiveness Data and Information Set published by the National Committee for Quality Assurance (NCQA).[9] The websites of most payers promote their best practices and share information about successes. You will want to evaluate the information that is publicly available and consider how your practice aligns with the values of the payer.

> **Example:** If a payer has information on its public website about a program for controlling diabetes by offering different supports and promoting its successes, putting forth a business proposal that supports achieving and maintaining control of diabetes is something already of interest to the payer. You can also consider the information in the light of what is not described. You may be able to gain traction with the payer by offering the ability to help manage another chronic condition so that the payer has another value statement that increases its competitive position. Much of the negotiation will depend upon the size of your practice and the relative strength of the proposal in terms of quality and cost.

Over 90% of health plans report HEDIS measures. Currently, HEDIS defines ninety-two measures across six domains of care with detailed specifications on how data is defined to ensure comparability of results between health plans for each measure. The health insurance plan ratings are posted on the NCQA website.[10] In reviewing the scores, consider how performance compares among your local payers and where scores rank. Any performance measures with lower scores are areas where the payer needs assistance. Depending on whether the payer contracts with employers or other purchasers like Medicaid, the payer may have financial incentives or penalties associated with performance for specified HEDIS measures. Often, a health plan creates a performance improvement plan to address quality measures that are not at appropriate levels. As a provider in the network, you may be able to gain access to a payer's quality improvement plan, which will provide greater insight to actions being taken to improve results. You can then evaluate how your practice can enhance the payer's performance.

You can also gather information by contacting your provider relations representative. If your initial contact is not able to provide information, escalate the call. Talking to the health plan network representative or someone higher up in the organization may provide ideas for specific areas of interest. Use that conversation also as an opportunity to gather information about how your practice compares to your peers. If reports are not available on the provider portal, request information about the cost and utilization of your practice versus other comparable practices for emergency room visits, inpatient hospitalizations, images and testing, prescriptions, and labs. Payers can also provide information on the risk scoring of your patients, top diagnoses, and average care cost per beneficiary. The health plan may also be willing to share data on costs across types of care and providers. Knowing the calculated costs allows for estimating potential savings to the health plan and building a case that overall savings will result, which offsets the payments made to your practice to transform how you deliver care and outcomes.

Rate Setting Process

When a health plan is pursuing new or renewal business, an actuarial review is performed to assess previous clinical costs as demonstrated by claims payments for medical, dental, prescription, laboratory, and other costs. Understanding how a health plan assesses risk can help you structure your process to assess your internal risk and prepare a meaningful business proposal for moving from FFS to value-based payments. At the very high-level overview, a health plan begins with information on the historical experience of the members or population being served. The experience is reviewed by examining characteristics of the population and claims experience.

The following are examples of characteristics associated with medical costs:

- Demographics
  - age, gender, and physical location
- Site of service
  - institutional (facility) or professional (physician and community-based)
- Type of service
  - evaluation and management, emergency department, inpatient
- Type and licensure of provider
  - primary care and cardiology, and physician, nurse practitioner, and psychologist
- Diagnosis or diagnostic related grouping
  - diabetes and hypertension
- Burden or severity of illness
  - the complexity of illness
- Unit cost
  - reimbursement per service or other payment mechanism
- Volume of services
  - usually defined in terms of visits, days, or admissions per 1,000
- Length of time in treatment
  - period for an episode of care

Analysis is completed using all available information to provide the clearest snapshot of the population as possible. After examining the historical experience, the health plan considers how costs can be altered by affecting utilization and reimbursement. For contracts where health plan capitation rates are set by an external actuary, such as in a Medicaid contract, a databook is prepared that provides information about the covered populations and services as well as any adjustments. The process is designed to allow for the actuary to conclude that rates are actuarially sound per generally accepted actuarial principles and practices.

When the actuaries set rates for Medicaid services, historical information is reviewed in a similar manner as will be done by health plans. Adjustments are made based on comparative data from other health plans or similar populations, national trends in indices i.e., the Consumer Price Index (CPI), external benchmarks, program changes, and assumptions about managed care controls. On top of the actual costs to deliver care, an administrative load is added to develop capitation rates. These rates are generally defined based on gender, age, and coverage group, with adjustments for locality and severity. Although there is a significant amount of data crunching associated with this process that is not detailed here, being able to align your business proposal with similar concepts allows you to speak the health plan's language and present results in a similar fashion.

Making an Appealing Business Case

In preparing a business proposal, write a one that provides an executive summary supported by detailed information. Your proposal needs to include not only your specific request but also needs to demonstrate the completeness of your analysis by defining the benefits, timing, assumptions, and any other high-level information supported by the financial analysis and rationale. How this information is presented matters. Keep the information factual, concise, and clearly identify support for your statements.

Request

The request is your specific "ask," or how you want to structure the value-based payment arrangement. Examples of initial requests to move to value-based payments include proposing a higher reimbursement for each service or adding a new service based on demonstrated outcomes.

MAKING THE BUSINESS CASE

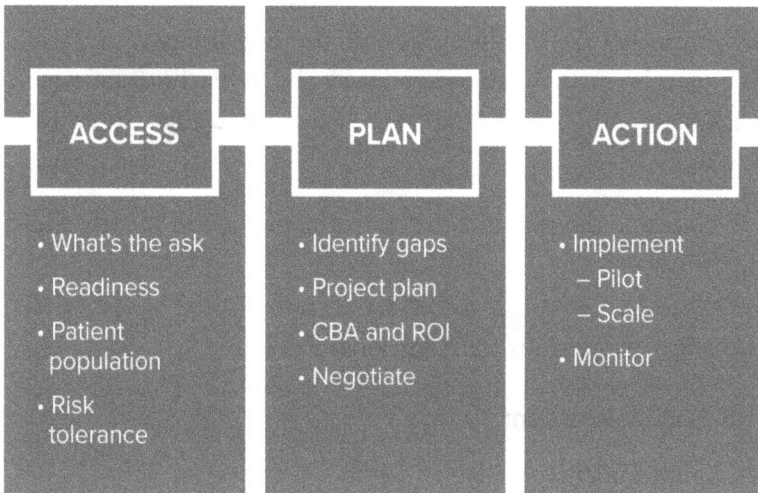

FIGURE 11.5 Making the Business Case

Identify the requested reimbursement and related terms. The field is wide open for what you ask as reimbursement.

A strong request ties the payment to claims submission. Claims are easy to bill for the provider and easy to process by a payer. An incentive payment for performing a health risk assessment is a simple example. The health risk assessment is billed with a specific code and the payer can process the claim as usual. The payer generates a system report reviewing the volume of health risk assessments that were billed and paid in the system.

Assume for this scenario that you negotiated a $4.50 payment per health risk assessment, with additional incentives based on completing assessments for higher percentages of eligible patients. Your initial baseline for health risk assessments was at 25% of all eligible patients. Your incentive is a rate increase to $5.00 if at least 70% of all eligible patients receive a health risk assessment and a rate increase to $5.50 if at least 90% of all eligible patients receive a health risk assessment.

Based on submitting claims, a report can be run to determine the actual number of assessments billed and paid. This would then be compared to your attributed patients. If the thresholds for the incentive are met, claims can either be re-adjudicated at the rate increase, or a separate payment can be made to the provider by the payer. Both parties should reconcile data to ensure agreement exists on claims submitted and processed.

To continue the example, below is the projection for the additional revenue:

TABLE 11.2:   Projections for Additional Revenue

Health Risk Assessment			
Total Eligible Patients	1,000		
Current HRA Patients	250		
Reimbursement	$ 4.50		
Current revenue	$ 1,125		
Projected HRA Patients	500	700	900
Reimbursement	$ 4.50	$ 5.00	$ 5.50
Projected revenue	$ 2,250	$ 3,500	$ 4,950
Current revenue	$ 1,125	$ 1,125	$ 1,125
Incremental revenue	$ 1,125	$ 2,375	$ 3,825

When crafting a position, evaluate the challenges with the payment mechanism from both your perspective as well as that of the health plan. The goal is to minimize administrative burden for both parties. Keep in mind that data will need to be provided to prove the achievement of the outcome, whether through a claim, encounter, or report. The more integrated the proof is with the current administrative processes, the easier it is to sell the idea.

Because a health plan has significantly more information than your organization about care about a specific person or population, ask for routine data as part of your proposal, and incorporate the use of that data into your monitoring processes. By receiving routine data, results can be monitored throughout the measurement period and any concerns or issues with the data can be identified early in the process. Waiting until the final calculations are made does not provide an opportunity for corrections.

One of the most commonly cited issues with HEDIS scores is the follow-up after an applicable inpatient hospitalization. As mentioned in Chapter 7, the HEDIS measure requires that people in certain populations (substance use or mental health issues) with an inpatient hospitalization be seen for a follow-up visit within 7 days of discharge. If your practice is looking to assist the health plan improve its scores, your practice needs to know when a patient has been admitted and discharged. As mentioned in Chapter 5, if an HIE is not available and your local hospital(s) will not provide ADT information directly, request that the health plan provide a notification. Having this information available in a useful format allows your practice to reach out to those that have recently been involved in higher levels of care.

Preparing Your Analysis

A detailed analysis should include both your internal information and any competitive information gathered externally. It must also include your projected revenues and expenses as well as any savings projected from changes in utilization of care. Internally, all the projections and related assumptions are shared to ensure a full discussion about risk and rewards. A more general treatment of the results of the analysis is shared externally when negotiating with payers or other stakeholders.

The key elements to document are the assumptions that were made in analyzing the changes. Be aware of the risk associated with each of the assumptions, particularly for instances where information is limited, and the assumptions push further into the category of "best guess." When summarizing the analysis, the assumptions need to clearly articulate how you arrived at the conclusion—and support how either savings or cost neutrality is achieved. As part of your analysis, some information is concretely quantified for known amounts like salaries and technology costs. But some factors of your analysis may be considered non-quantifiable. These factors are difficult to tag to either revenue or cost. Examples of these intangible factors are your competitiveness and positioning in the marketplace. For these factors, estimating a change in revenue offers the opportunity to evaluate potential increases or decreases based on a decision. Using a range of potential impacts allows for developing a sensitivity analysis where you examine the outcome based on changes to assumptions. Prepare the sensitivity analysis by creating financial scenarios based on varying your assumptions. In the previous example of payment for a health risk assessment, your sensitivity analysis could show the difference in the finance results (revenue, cost, and profit) based on the differing levels of completed HRAs (500, 700, 900), similar to how the example is displayed.

Another part of your analysis and preparation for presentation is to develop counterarguments. To evaluate potential opposing arguments, consider the reasons why the decision is wrong and challenge your assumptions. This helps to define areas where your information is strong, and assumptions are clear. For areas where assumptions were less definitive, be specific about the basis for your estimate and be honest about the uncertainty.

Negotiating

When negotiating with a payer or health plan, start with a value proposition. Your value proposition is a statement that clearly defines the benefit to the health plan and is followed by a summary that identifies key elements and any assumptions.

Your written proposal should clearly define the proposed value-based payment arrangement and what savings the health plan can anticipate. Supporting your written statement with financial analysis provides the health plan the opportunity to evaluate how savings were derived. Savings calculated on data provided by that health plan will have the most impact. While generating savings is preferred, a proposal that is cost neutral or even potentially costing more can also be attractive. Remember, the health plans may have additional sources to fund your payments, like incentives for achieving certain HEDIS goals.

When stating reimbursement terms, comparisons to Medicare rates tend to be standard. Many health plans negotiate rates as a percentage of Medicare. But in some markets, a comparison to published Medicaid rates may be more applicable. Mirroring that language makes the analysis by health plan analysis easier to accomplish and creates a comparable base. Unless the scope of your organization is broad or includes a hospital, savings may well be generated outside of your practice. The health plans are concerned about the cost of emergency department utilization, avoidable hospitalizations, and readmissions. Positively impacting any of those costs can create a winning scenario for health plans.

The negotiation for value-based payments is likely to span a several months. Unless a specific program is already established by a payer and accepted as presented, your practice will be involved in negotiating the terms and answering questions about the proposal and analysis. Information presented will be vetted by the health plan by reviewing claims history of your practice as well as information about other services consumed by members covered under the terms of your proposal.

When considering the timing of this part of the process, anticipate meetings to describe the proposal, communicate supporting facts and assumptions, and respond to questions from the payer. Even after agreement in principle is reached, the proposal must be converted into contractual language. Ensure that the contract is clear about specific measures, reimbursements, timing, and any reporting, auditing or other monitoring. Any reports or other data and information based between both parties will need to be validated. Make sure to include contractual language that addresses data discrepancies and requires reconciliations. Also include language that addresses any issues with acceptance of claims or encounters if the value-based care measures involve calculations based on them.

During the interactions with the health plan or payer, always push for a follow-up date or point of decision. The goal is to keep both parties engaged and keep momentum.

CHAPTER 12

Keeping the Momentum

After working through a transition, your practice needs to focus on maintaining improvements, continuing to evolve your patient-centered approach, and delivering values-based care. Incorporating continuous quality improvement as a way of doing business ensures that the focus stays on the patient, improving outcomes, and maximizing reimbursement under value-based care. By tracking and trending your performance, you stay focused on setting goals for higher levels of performance.

According to the National Academy of Medicine, formerly called the Institute of Medicine, quality is defined as "the degree to which health services for individuals and populations increase the likelihood of desired health outcomes and are consistent with current professional knowledge."[1] As described in Chapter 1, the goal of value-based care is to satisfy six aims: safe, effective, patient-centered, timely, efficient, and equitable care.

These six aims can be used as a guide to determine if the outcomes and quality improvement activities are appropriate. Most issues in quality come from underuse, overuse, or misuse of resources.[2] Establish a quality improvement program and incorporate the mentality of looking for ways to improve. By keeping the focus on outcomes and values, your practice will move in the right direction.

Establishing Quality Improvement

Throughout your transformation process, you work to change the culture of your practice and promote an environment of learning and not placing blame. As part of this culture shift, everyone on your teams becomes more comfortable with data, measuring performance, assessing what went well, and identifying what can be improved.

As you move toward embedding quality improvement into your organization, use pilot programs when establishing new goals and implementing interventions. Pilots start on a smaller scale, are easier to manage, and allow for corrections along the way. As noted during the change process, you can also create short-term wins to demonstrate how the changes improve outcomes. This helps to gain buy-in and support by those affected by the changes. When working through this process, be sure to communicate that additional changes, whether corrections or tweaks, are normal. Quality improvement is an iterative process. It is okay when things do not work the first time. The culture and environment need to support successes and failures. By starting on a smaller scale, failures tend to have reduced consequences.

To be successful, quality improvement needs dedicated resources, even if it is not a full-time staff position. These resources include policies and procedures to sustain quality improvement (QI) goals as well as staff time or positions involved in quality improvement teams and regular meetings to discuss QI activities. Form a QI team to be responsible for oversight and managing the process, but ownership should be held by everyone within your practice. The QI team shapes and prioritizes areas for improvement. This includes defining specific measures for improving patient health, population health, and practice performance.

At the center of quality improvement is data. Using data allows for an assessment of how your practice is currently performing, identifying and setting targets with related interventions or changes and determining the effectiveness of those changes. The QI team is responsible for the collection and analysis of the data. But the information should not remain with just that team. Results are to be shared throughout the practice and successes shared to further solidify a culture of quality. You will use the success of the pilot programs to support wider implementation.

There is a saying that "what gets measured gets done." Proof of this adage can be found in many places. In an article written by the *Kaiser Family Foundation*, the results from Medicare requiring measures about three conditions have resulted in decreased readmissions. In 2012, the Hospital Readmission Reduction Program instituted penalties for readmissions for heart failure, heart attack, and pneumonia. With the introduction of penalties, lower readmission rates resulted. According to the article, the lower readmission rates suggest systemwide improvements have occurred.[3]

Models for Quality Improvement

In determining the best model for your practice, you need to consider complexity and resources. For smaller practices, a simple model that focuses on measuring performance, assessing attainment of goals, and areas to improve may be enough. For larger practices or organizations with more resources, quality improvement is a dedicated department, staffed with positions with specific roles and responsibilities. In either case, your practice should have a model for assessing quality improvement and the related activities. The goal is to have qualitative data to identify, inform, and evaluate improvement activities and efforts. Models frequently cited for structuring healthcare quality improvement are Six Sigma®, Lean, Lean Six Sigma, and The Model for Improvement.

Six Sigma®

Six Sigma Beautiful! is based on the concept that waste results from variation in the process. Six Sigma has its roots as a management standard in the 18th century work of Carl Friedrich Gauss defining a normal curve. In the 1920s, Walter Shewhart determined that three sigma (or standard deviations) from the mean required correction. The concept of the standard deviation identifies variation from the mean, or what is normal. Six Sigma was developed by Motorola in the 1980s and measured defects per million opportunities instead of the former standard of thousands of opportunities. The definition of Six Sigma is variation of less than or equal to 3.4 defects per million units created. [4]

Lean and Lean Six Sigma

Whereas Six Sigma asserts that all process variations cause waste, Lean thinking asserts that waste occurs due to unnecessary steps in a process that do not add value. Lean is derived from the Toyota Production System.

Five core principles define Lean:

- Value
  - based on the customer's needs
- Value stream
  - actions needed to deliver the service
- Flow
  - process flows smoothly
- Pull
  - responding to customer needs and only moving to the next step when ready
- Perfection
  - absence of defects, focusing on continuous quality improvement[5]

Based on the five principles, meeting customer expectations is required. Value or quality is derived when what is delivered exceeds customer expectations.

A variation that combines principles from Six Sigma and Lean is known as Lean Six Sigma. With Lean Six Sigma, the focus is on the

LEAN PRINCIPLES

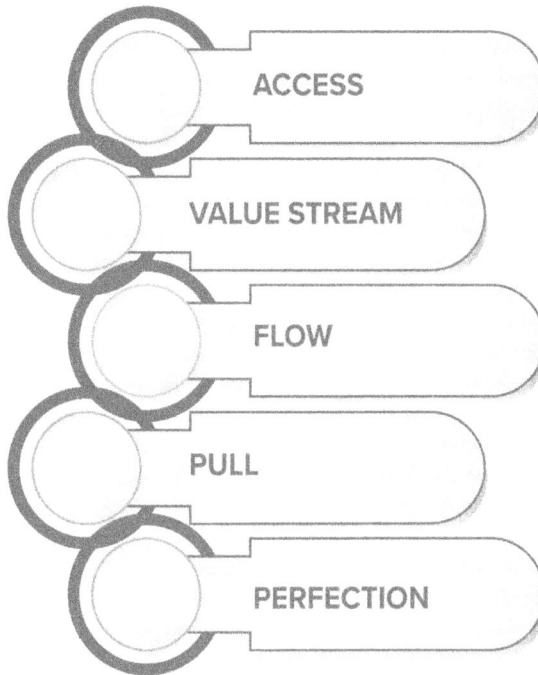

ACCESS

VALUE STREAM

FLOW

PULL

PERFECTION

FIGURE 12.1   Lean Principles

customer, not the process. The definition of a customer is very broad and should not be thought of as just the patient but rather whoever is the next individual involved in any defined process. In an office encounter, the workflow is begun by a medical assistant rooming a patient, followed by the physician who is armed with information beforehand. In this scenario, the customer of the medical assistant is not only the patient but also the physician.

In Lean Six Sigma, waste is the result of D.O.W.N.T.I.M.E.

- Defects
  - These are mistakes that require additional time resources or money; incomplete or inaccurate information in products or services such as charts or patient registrations.

- Overproduction
  - Results from making too much, too early, or faster than needed, such as prepping an injection and not being able to use it.
- Waiting
  - Needing information, materials, or people, such as waiting on the phone for a consult or preauthorization, or unbalanced workloads.
- Non-utilized talent
  - Not using skills, knowledge, and experience of those involved in the process, such as not including the patient in care planning, not delegating responsibilities, and poor communication.
- Transportation
  - Unnecessary movement of items or information, such as moving supplies between locations.
- Inventory
  - When supply within the process is greater than customer need or demand, such as excess supplies or vaccines.
- Motion
  - Unnecessary movement of people, such as walking an unnecessary distance to inconveniently located printers.
- Extra processing
  - Performing any action that does not add value, such as obtaining multiple signatures or approvals.[6]

Lean and Six Sigma both use a process to define the approach to quality improvement. Below is an overview of how Lean Six Sigma defines the steps in the process:

- Define
  - Understand your customer and their requirements, problems, and goals, and a high-level view of the process.

- Measure
  - Map the current process, determine current performance, look for potential sources of problems or waste, create a plan for data collection, and ensure data is reliable.
- Analyze
  - Identify the root cause of the problem through data analysis.
- Improve
  - Implement and verify the solution after considering alternatives and measure the effectiveness of an improvement.
- Control
  - Maintain the improvement, work toward continuous improvement by managing and monitoring the process, share knowledge, and celebrate success.[7]

DMAIC PROCESS

D	M	A	I	C
Define	Measure	Analyze	Improve	Control

FIGURE 12.2   DMAIC

Implementing Lean Six Sigma in your organization will be maximized if practice staff can pursue education and training. Certifications exist for both Lean Six Sigma and Six Sigma.

The Model for Improvement

A simple model that is promoted by the IHI is the Model for Improvement. Created by the Associates in Process Improvement, the Model for Improvement is designed to accelerate improvement within an organization. The IHI has a helpful Quality Improvement Essentials Toolkit on its website. It includes worksheets and project plans that will help practices implement programs based on this model.[8] The model is based on three central questions along with implementation of the plan-do-study-act (PDSA) cycle.[9] These three questions create a focus for improvement efforts:

- What are we trying to accomplish?
- How will we know that a change is an improvement?
- What change can we make that will result in improvement?

After answering these three questions, the PDSA cycle is implemented for the specific improvement. The cycle of planning, doing, studying, and acting is a never-ending loop. Often depicted as a continuous circle, the stages begin with planning. The fourth stage of acting leads back into planning as part of the iterative, continuous quality improvement process.

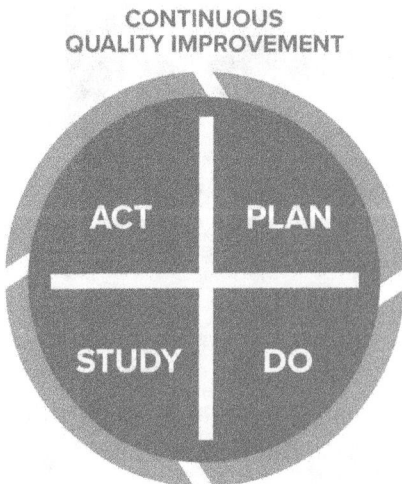

FIGURE 12.3   The Model for Improvement © Jossey-Bass (Wiley)

Plan

The first stage of an improvement cycle is the planning phase. This stage involves creating a plan for testing an observation, including defining data that will be collected, and a strategy for the overall cycle.

When first initiating this stage, your practice should identify the goal or purpose of the improvement activity and prepare for the next phases. A well-documented, written action plan is the deliverable for the planning stage. Your action plan should include the following components:

- Objective or area of focus
- Current baseline or other measure of performance (and related dates of this baseline measurement period)
- Specific and measurable goals
- Brief description of actions or interventions
- Start date of interventions and actions
- Resources needed to implement initiatives (including identification of the leader)
- Potential barriers and options to overcoming them
- Measurements of progress and success (including how and when measurements will be taken)
- Specific workflows and individuals affected by the change
- Timelines with specific start dates for tasks and actions
- Communication and distribution plan for sharing actions and results

When reviewing options for improvements, assessing and weighing the value of actions assists the process of prioritizing resources. Some QI activities may provide a competitive advantage or have technical merit for your practice that outweighs other considerations. However, when in the planning stage, seeking input from those affected by potential changes allows for better insights. Gathering information from those directly involved also helps to avoid choosing an intervention that will not fix the actual problem. Individuals involved in a process targeted for improvement often already have insight into needed changes.

During the planning stage, be sure to communicate with staff how information will be collected and why it is important. If the quality improvement activity is aligned with value-based care, you should be able to describe how the change and related data improves quality, outcomes, and the patient experience of care.

To avoid administrative burden and information overload, start with a small number of measures that are manageable. Make sure the measures collect enough information and allow for determining if a targeted change is effective. This is accomplished by using more than one measure associated with the activity. For example, in a primary care practice measuring outcomes associated with diabetes, select measures that include more than rates of patients with good control of blood sugar levels (A1c <9). Related measures for diabetic care include rates of nephropathy screenings, rate of retinal/eye exams, and rates for foot exams. In this scenario, by expanding the number of measures associated with diabetes, your practice develops a broader understanding of services that are designed to test appropriate care for patients diagnosed with diabetes.

Do

The next phase of the improvement cycle is implementation of the activity on a small scale or pilot basis. During this stage, document observations including any problems or unexpected results. Perform an initial analysis of the data to determine if changes to the intervention need to be made. The observations may identify unanticipated barriers. The small scale allows for changes to be made when overcoming challenges and roadblocks.

During this stage, only make changes that are necessary. Consistency in the action phase makes the analysis phase easier to assess the effect of change. If any corrections are made to the process outside of the formalized planning, document what the changes are and when they were implemented. Otherwise, determining cause and effect may be difficult when analyzing the results in the next step of the process.

Continuing the primary care example of measures related to diabetic care, in the implementation phase the practice would implement the specific actions to increase the number of individuals being screened for nephropathy and having eye and foot exams. The actions that practices may take could include creating a registry of individuals diagnosed with diabetes, and performing an outreach campaign through mail, e-mail, or phone contact. When tracking actions during a PDSA cycle, ensure specific actions occur after the baseline time period. The actions would be ongoing through the initial measurement period. Examples of specific time periods are:

- Baseline period: January to June 2019
- Intervention initiated: July 2019 (outreach campaign implemented)
- Remeasurement period: July to December 2019

Study

In the third phase, data and datasets are analyzed and results are studied. Aggregate the data and compare it to the original goals and predictions. Summarize results and document insights. This includes evaluating the effectiveness of the interventions and verifying the validity of results. The result of the study phase is drawing conclusions about the effectiveness of actions taken.

When analyzing the results of actions taken by the primary care practice in the example case, data is collected to identify the following:

- Number of patients diagnosed with diabetes
- Volume of outreach activities (such as number of phone calls made, and e-mails or letters sent)
- Success of outreach contact (such as the number of phone calls answered)
- Rates of the specific measures (nephropathy screenings, foot exams, and eye exams) during the time period of intervention

The rates of the specific measures would then be compared to the rates of the baseline period. If the improvement period rates are better than the baseline rates, then improvement is demonstrated. This comparison should also be made against the defined goals. In some cases, although improvement maybe demonstrated, goals may not be met.

Continuing the diabetes example, the following chart displays of the hypothetical results:

TABLE 12.1   Calculating Average Cost of a Patient Visit

Measure	Baseline	Goal	Initial Measurement
Nephropathy screening	15%	50%	35%
Foot exams	25%	50%	55%
Eye exams	40%	50%	35%

The analysis of these results indicates that although improvement was achieved for two of the three measures, only foot exams achieved the established goal. The eye exams show a decrease in performance.

Act

The fourth stage of the process improvement cycle is to reassess and respond. By examining the data, an assessment of what worked and what did not is completed. Use this information in the upcoming planning stage, when the process improvement cycle repeats. During this phase, successful changes are shared and incorporated in other parts of the organization.

To conclude the sample case of the primary care practice measuring performance associated with diabetic care, in the fourth phase the practice determines what changes should be made to further impact performance. For the nephropathy screening, the initial goal of 50% was not met. The practice then must evaluate options for additional actions that can be taken to achieve the goal. Maybe this includes targeted outreach and further education about the importance of nephropathy screening. Or possibly the practice may collect urine samples in the office, or schedule lab visits for a patient as part of the discharge process.

During this phase of the PDSA cycle, ideas for new actions or modifications of existing actions are generated to be used in the next planning phase. The same type of process occurs for actions associated with the eye exams and possibly even with the foot exams. The practice could choose to increase the goal for foot exams for the next PDSA cycle to continue improving care.

Sharing Results

As part of delivering on continuous quality improvement, information about the process as well as the established goals and results should be shared throughout the office. To strengthen the team identity, the team should understand the goals, why they are important, and see progress along the way.

In this concept of team, share the information with all members of the office, not just the treating provider or clinical care team. The information can be shared using a variety of methods. Results of efforts can be shared through e-mail, in meetings, and posted in a common location. Additionally, if you are sharing results with your patients, you can post information in the waiting area, on the website, during the patient and family council meetings, and any other place where the patients are likely to view the information. The data can also be shared publicly by reporting to independent sources or participating in registries.

When implementing any quality improvement initiatives, you are likely to experience barriers to change. In addition to change resistance, you may also encounter structural or resource issues. As was addressed during the transformation process, adequate staffing and IT systems, training in quality improvement, and supportive policies and procedures are required.

All the issues identified in gaining cooperation and buy-in from staff and patients to accomplish transformation efforts also applies to implementing continuous quality improvement. By its very nature, continuous quality improvement necessitates change. Resistance to change and pushback are normal and should be expected. However, if your transformation process has fostered a sense of innovation and the pursuit of continuous improvement, the culture will provide positive reinforcement to the concept of change. To fully implement value-based care, your practice must adopt a continuous quality improvement approach. Choosing which model works best for your organization is based on your resources and the level of complexity that can be managed.

Third Party Accreditation or Recognition

For some practices, obtaining third party recognition or accreditation provides a competitive advantage or could even be a requirement to participate in value-based payment programs. To meet the requirements of an independent certification, a quality improvement function (like the one outlined in the previous section) is necessary. Accreditation or recognition involves meeting the defined standards or criteria as developed by an independent organization. Achieving the standards is promoted as evidence that the practice delivers quality services and follows appropriate clinical protocols. The standards or criteria create a framework and guidance for practices to follow. To obtain and maintain any accreditation or recognition, however, requires engaging in a process that lays a foundation that incorporates elements to meet the criteria. Over a period of time, as the foundation becomes stronger, your practice will have the flexibility to become more sophisticated and be able to meet future criteria. Revisions to independent accreditation standards move participants toward more complex and advanced criteria.

Working toward accreditation can provide an end goal that drives focus and helps to build and sustain momentum. One word of caution is to ensure that your practice does not become solely focused on merely obtaining the accreditation approval score. Seeking accreditation can lead to a fixation about achieving a certain score in the standards and create a checklist mentality. To succeed and maintain accreditation, the philosophy and the goals that accreditation represents must be embraced by the organization. Understanding why you are pursuing accreditation and transforming your practice is just as important, if not more so, than implementing new processes or changes to existing workflows. Accreditation should be looked at as icing on the cake, not the cake itself.

The benefits of obtaining and maintaining accreditation must be weighed against the costs. Some of the benefits of accreditation include:

- Create a competitive advantage.
- Strengthen the focus on patient outcomes and safety.
- Reduce risk of errors and poor quality.
- Make a strong statement to patients, staff, and the public about the importance that your practice places on quality.
- Potentially reduce the cost of liability insurance.
- Foster education and professional development for staff.
- Provide a framework for organizing the structure, management, and delivery of care.
- Meet regulatory and/or payer requirements.
- Strengthen performance and deliver better health outcomes.
- Reduce costs by eliminating unnecessary work.

Quantifying the benefits listed above may be difficult, but they are worth assessing when considering whether to pursue accreditation. Like analyzing the costs and benefits of implementing a value-based care model with APMs, a scenario for pursuing accreditation has to be evaluated. In some cases, payers incentivize practices to attain accreditation by either providing funding to obtain the accreditation or increasing reimbursement after the accreditation is achieved. In other cases, the lack of independent accreditation may be a barrier to participating in APMs. In that situation, if your practice does not obtain accreditation, it will be penalized and excluded.

When determining whether to pursue accreditation, the first step is to gather information about the requirements and costs. Compare how your current performance complies with the standards and identify the gaps in processes. The next step is to assess the resources needed to change operations to meet the standards. This involves identifying not only resources but also a timeline for implementation deadlines. Depending on your level of knowledge, contracting for external assistance may help facilitate the assessment and identification of necessary actions. Obtaining accreditation will likely take longer than you anticipate unless you are already in the process of transforming your practice.

As a rule, transitioning processes and implementing a new quality improvement process takes a *minimum* of six months. This amount of time is the shortest window recommended for determining if changes have resulted in improvement. Having the ability to demonstrate a quality improvement process is required under most independent accreditation standards. The need to develop this process may help define the minimum amount of time to prepare for accreditation. Consideration must be given for any processes or workflows that need to be established to support the quality improvement efforts. The cycle to prepare for accreditation can take anywhere from six months to two years or more. The length of time will depend on your starting point in terms of current compliance with standards and available resources as well as the level of support from leadership.

The Joint Commission and NCQA are the most widely recognized accreditation organizations. Other accrediting bodies offer programs that may be more tailored to a specific practice type, such as the Commission on Accreditation of Rehabilitation Facilities (CARF International), the Council on Accreditation (COA), and the Accreditation Association of Ambulatory Healthcare (AAAHC). To decide which accreditation is best for you practice, consider the costs and resources needed to obtain the accreditation. But also consider the reputation of the accrediting organizations and the value in the eyes of stakeholders, including payers, patients, and staff. In some states, only certain accrediting bodies are recognized to qualify for incentives and funding.

The Joint Commission

The Joint Commission offers multiple versions of accreditation standards, including ambulatory care, hospital, critical access hospital, and behavioral healthcare. The Joint Commission standards are designed to promote health equity and patient-centered care. For practices that have a relationship with a facility that is accredited by TJC, pursuing accreditation for ambulatory care may be easier.

A practice must meet eligibility criteria in order to qualify for accreditation. The accreditation process involves an on-site review to determine compliance with standards. Joint Commission utilizes a tracer methodology which follows an actual patient through the entire healthcare process. After obtaining accreditation, a practice or facility is eligible to obtain additional certifications. These certifications include:

- Integrated Care
- Comprehensive Cardiac Center
- Disease-Specific Care in 18 categories such as cardiovascular, orthopedics, or pulmonary
- Health Care Staffing Services
- Medication Compounding
- Palliative Care
- Perinatal Care
- Patient Blood Management
- Primary Care Medical Home (PCMH)

As of April 26, 2018, The Joint Commission identified over 236 accredited organizations with 1,776 sites. More information about accreditation and recognition by The Joint Commission can be found at www.jointcommission.org.

NCQA

Accreditation, certification, and recognition programs are offered by NCQA. For most ambulatory care practices, recognition programs are the most appropriate. Eligibility requirements are defined by the specific type of recognition program. In general, NCQA updates the standards for recognition every three years. The standards and guidelines are available on the NCQA website. In 2018, the recognition programs include:

- Patient-Centered Medical Home (PCMH)
- Patient-Centered Specialty Practice (PCSP)
- Oncology Medical Home
- Patient-Centered Connected Care
- School-Based Medical Home
- Government Recognition Initiative

Additionally, NCQA offers distinction programs for behavioral health integration and patient experience reporting. Programs that recognize individual clinicians include those for diabetes and heart/ stroke. The review process performed by NCQA is completed off-site. With the introduction of the PCMH 2017 standards, reviews are virtual, with screen sharing between the evaluator and the practice. During the virtual review, the practice can show reports, systems, schedules, and other documentation that provides evidence of meeting the standards. More information regarding NCQA recognition can be found at www. ncqa.org.

Continuous Quality Improvement Culture

Adopting a quality improvement approach assists your practice in maintaining changes achieved during the transformation process. At the heart of quality improvement is a focus on data, which is also central to a value-based care organization. Your efforts to transition your practice should result in a culture that embraces data-informed and data-driven continuous improvement.

Working through a continuous quality improvement process, your practice will be restructured to be more efficient and effective at achieving patient and population health outcomes. These changes must be tested and studied to determine if modifications are needed. Your organization or practice may also want to consider pursuing accreditation or recognition from an independent organization. Just be sure that you understand why you are transitioning how your practice operates and resist getting caught up in the checklist mentality.

CHAPTER 13

In Conclusion

Dear Reader,

You chose healthcare because you want to *help* people be healthy. This is still the end goal, despite what may seem like chaos swirling around the system.

Trust in your values, know your strengths, and capitalize on them. Adapting to change is an essential skill when living in a fast-paced, technology-driven world that is connected 24/7.

The pace will not slow.

Understand the basics and move your organization in the direction needed: survival of the fittest requires adaptation. Some of this is the driving force behind consolidations and integrations, whether vertical or horizontal. Everyone is looking to control the playing field. Yes, large practices need to change—but even small practices need to change to survive.

You've taken the first step to moving forward. Incremental steps lead to significant change in the long run. Adopting an approach of continuous improvement that reflects your values will help you succeed.

You can do more than just weather the latest changes. You can create a vision of a healthier world and boldly lead others to healthcare that embodies quality and value by delivering care in a way that reflects your values.

Stand by your values, remember why your practice exists, and how you benefit your patients and community. Use your values to guide your activities and motivate your staff to transform. Everyone wins. And when everyone wins it means rewards, success, affirmation of your career choice and a healthier patient population, community, and world.

I wish you the best in your journey.

-Jennifer

Reference Notes and Resources

Chapter 1 Getting Ahead of The Curve

1 Daryl Pritchard, PhD et al., "What Contributes Most to High Health Care Costs? Health Care Spending in High Resource Patients," *Journal of Managed Care & Specialty Pharmacy,* February 2016, https://doi.org/10.18553/jmcp.2016.22.2.102.

2 Roy Beveridge, et al., "Humana Value Report Shows Progress for Medicare Advantage Members Affiliated with Providers in Value-Based Care Agreements," Humana Healthcare, November 13, 2018, https://press.humana.com/press-release/current-releases/humana-value-report-shows-progress-medicare-advantage-members-affilia.

3 *Crossing the Quality Chasm: A New Health System for the 21st Century,* Institute of Medicine (US) Committee on Quality of Health Care in America, National Academies Press (US), Vol 2, *Improving the 21st-century Health Care System*, accessed June 6, 2019, available from: https://www.ncbi.nlm.nih.gov/books/NBK222265/.

4 "The IHI Triple Aim," Institute for Healthcare Improvement, January 26, 2018, accessed June 6, 2019, http://www.ihi.org/Engage/Initiatives/TripleAim/Pages/default.aspx.

5 Thomas Bodenheimer and Christine Sinsky, "From Triple to Quadruple Aim: Care of the Patient Requires Care of the Provider," *Annals of Family Medicine,* November 01, 2014, accessed March 13, 2019. http://www.annfammed.org/content/12/6/573.full.

6 Derek Feeley, "The Triple Aim or The Quadruple Aim? Four Points to Help Set Your Strategy," *Improvement Blog,* Institute for Healthcare Improvement, November 28, 2017, accessed June 7, 2019, http://www.ihi.org/communities/blogs/the-triple-aim-or-the-quadruple-aim-four-points-to-help-set-your-strategy.

7 "Delivery System Reform Incentive Payment (DSRIP) program," New York Department of Health, last modified April 2019, https://www.health.ny.gov/health_care/medicaid/redesign/dsrip/.

8 "Section 223 Demonstration Program for Certified Community Behavioral Health Clinics," SAMHSA, last modified October 11, 2019, https://www.samhsa.gov/section-223.

9 "Oncology Care Model," Center for Medicare & Medicaid Innovation, last modified June 3, 2019, https://innovation.cms.gov/initiatives/oncology-care/.

10 "Accountable Care Organizations (ACOs): General Introduction," Center for Medicare & Medicaid Innovation, last modified June 3, 2019, https://innovation.cms.gov/initiatives/aco/.

11 "Bundled Payments for Care Improvement (BPCI) Initiative: General Information," Center for Medicare & Medicaid Innovation, last updated April 17, 2019, https://innovation.cms.gov/initiatives/bundled-payments/.

12 "MACRA: MIPS & APMs," Centers for Medicare & Medicaid Services, last modified September 21, 2018, https://www.cms.gov/medicare/quality-initiatives-patient-assessment-instruments/value-based-programs/macra-mips-and-apms/macra-mips-and-apms.html.

13 Sonia Thompson, "How Nike, Disney, and the Ritz Carlton Built Cultures That Always Deliver Great Customer Experiences," *Inc.com*, accessed June 7, 2019, https://www.inc.com/sonia-thompson/how-nike-disney-ritz-carlton-built-cultures-that-always-deliver-great-customer-experiences.html.

Chapter 2: First Steps to Making Change Meaningful and Achievable

1 Christian Green, "A Healthy Organizational Culture Can Spur Success," MGMA, accessed June 11, 2019, https://www.mgma.com/data/data-stories/a-healthy-organizational-culture-can-spur-clinical.

2 "Chronic Diseases in America," National Center for Chronic Disease Prevention and Health Promotion (NCCDPHP), Centers for Disease Control and Prevention (CDC), last reviewed April 15, 2019, https://www.cdc.gov/chronicdisease/resources/infographic/chronic-diseases.htm.

3 Travis Bradberry, "9 Things That Make Good Employees Quit," *Inc.com*, accessed June 7, 2019, https://www.inc.com/travis-bradberry/9-things-that-make-good-employees-quit.html.

4 Javier Martinez, "Assessing Quality, Outcome and Performance Management," accessed June 7, 2019, https://www.who.int/hrh/documents/en/Assessing_quality.pdf.

5 Scott Brum, "What Impact Does Training Have on Employee Commitment and Employee Turnover?" University of Rhode Island digitalcommons@

uri, accessed June 7, 2019, https://digitalcommons.uri.edu/cgi/viewcontent.cgi?article=1022&context=lrc_paper_series.

6 "AHRQ Health Literacy Universal Precautions Toolkit, 2nd Edition," Agency for Healthcare Research and Quality (AHRQ), content last reviewed August 2018, https://www.ahrq.gov/professionals/quality-patient-safety/quality-resources/tools/literacy-toolkit/index.html.

7 "CHPL Overview," Certified Health IT (CHPL), accessed June 7, 2019 https://chpl.healthit.gov/#/resources/overview.

8 "Section 4: Ways to Approach the Quality Improvement Process," Agency for Healthcare Research and Quality (AHRQ), last reviewed March 2019, https://www.ahrq.gov/cahps/quality-improvement/improvement-guide/4-approach-qi-process/index.html.

9 Dean H. Gesme and Marian Wiseman, "Performance Appraisal: A Tool for Practice Improvement," *Journal of Oncology Practice*, March 1, 2011, https://ascopubs.org/doi/full/10.1200/JOP.2010.000214.

10 "6 Performance Management Tools for The Modern HR Department," ERC, accessed June 7, 2019, https://www.yourerc.com/blog/post/6-performance-management-tools-for-the-modern-hr-department.

11 "Module 14 Trainer's Guide: Creating Quality Improvement Teams and QI Plans," Agency for Healthcare Research and Quality (AHRQ), last reviewed May 2013, https://www.ahrq.gov/professionals/prevention-chronic-care/improve/system/pfhandbook/mod14trainers.html.

12 Gale Pryor, "Hitting Performance Targets with Data Transparency," athenahealth, accessed June 7, 2019, https://www.athenahealth.com/insight/data-transparency-healthcare-performance.

13 Tayfun Arar, et al., " Developing Competitive Strategies Based on SWOT Analysis in Porter s Five Forces Model by DANP," *Journal of Business Research*, accessed June 7, 2019, https://www.researchgate.net/publication/318043214.

14 Ronda G. Hughes, "Chapter 44 Tools and Strategies for Quality Improvement and Patient Safety," *Patient Safety and Quality: An Evidence-Based Handbook for Nurses,* Agency for Healthcare Research and Quality (US), April 2008, available from: https://www.ncbi.nlm.nih.gov/books/NBK2682/.

15 "Types of Health Care Quality Measures," Agency for Healthcare Research and Quality (AHRQ), accessed June 7, 2019, http://www.ahrq.gov/talkingquality/measures/types.html.

16 "Strategies for Measuring the Quality of Psychotherapy: A White Paper to Inform Measure Development and Implementation. IV. Structure Measures," Office of The Assistant Secretary for Planning & Evaluation, U.S. Department of Health & Human Services, accessed June 7, 2019, https://aspe.hhs.gov/report/strategies-measuring-quality-psychotherapy-white-paper-inform-measure-development-and-implementation/iv-structure-measures.

17 "Types of Health Care Quality Measures," Agency for Healthcare Research and Quality (AHRQ), accessed June 7, 2019, http://www.ahrq.gov/talkingquality/measures/types.html.

18 Caitlin Morris and Kim Bailey, "Measuring Health Care Quality: An Overview of Quality Measures," accessed June 7, 2019, Families USA, https://familiesusa.org/sites/default/files/product_documents/HSI%20Quality%20Measurement_Brief_final_web.pdf.

19 "Quality Positioning System," National Quality Forum, accessed June 7, 2019, http://www.qualityforum.org/QPS.

Chapter 3: Transforming Requires Leadership

1 Delorese Ambrose, *Managing Complex Change*, 1987, http://www.maximizingexcellence.org/application/files/8815/2174/3951/Managing_Complex_Change.pdf.

2 Sara Pollock, "Final Destination: Organizational Transparency," *Clear Company (blog)*, accessed June 7, 2019, https://blog.clearcompany.com/final-destination-organizational-transparency.

3 Michael Chui, et al., "The Social Economy: Unlocking Value and Productivity Through Social Technologies," McKinsey Global Institute, accessed June 7, 2019, https://www.mckinsey.com/~/media/McKinsey/Industries/High%20Tech/Our%20Insights/The%20social%20economy/MGI_The_social_economy_Full_report.ashx.

4 Amy Rees Anderson, "Successful Business Communication: It Starts at the Beginning," *Forbes.com*, accessed June 7, 2019, https://www.forbes.com/sites/

amyanderson/2013/05/28/successful-business-communication-it-starts-at-the-beginning/#461cd371db56.

Chapter 4: What Do Your Patients Have in Common?

1 David Kindig and Greg Stoddart, "What is Population Health?" *American Journal of Public Health (AJPH)*, October 10, 2011, https://ajph. aphapublications.org/doi/10.2105/AJPH.93.3.380.

2 Ibid.

3 Ibid.

4 "Office of Management and Budget (OMB), Directive No. 15, Race and Ethnic Standards for Federal Statistics and Administrative Reporting (as adopted on May 12, 1977)," CDC WONDER, last reviewed January 5, 2016, https://wonder.cdc.gov/wonder/help/populations/bridged-race/directive15. html.

5 Samantha Artiga and Elizabeth Hinton, " Beyond Health Care: The Role of Social Determinants in Promoting Health and Health Equity - Issue Brief," The Henry J. Kaiser Family Foundation, accessed June 7, 2019, https://www. kff.org/report-section/beyond-health-care-the-role-of-social-determinants-in-promoting-health-and-health-equity-issue-brief/.

Chapter 5: Understanding the Whole Picture of Patient Health

1 " Humana Value Report Shows Progress for Medicare Advantage Members Affiliated with Providers in Value-based Care Agreements," Humana Healthcare, November 13, 2018, https://press.humana.com/press-release/current-releases/humana-value-report-shows-progress-medicare-advantage-members-affilia.

2 "The State Innovation Models (SIM) Program: A Look at Round 2 Grantees," The Kaiser Commission on Medicaid and the Uninsured, The Henry J. Kaiser Family Foundation, accessed June 7, 2019, https://www.kff.org/medicaid/fact-sheet/the-state-innovation-models-sim-program-a-look-at-round-2-grantees/.

3 "PRAPARE: Protocol for Responding to and Assessing Patients' Assets, Risks, and Experiences," National Association of Community Health Centers (NACHC), accessed June 7, 2019, http://www.nachc.org/research-and-data/prapare/.

4 "Substance Use and Mental Health," National Institute of Mental Health (NIMH), accessed June 7, 2019, https://www.nimh.nih.gov/health/topics/substance-use-and-mental-health/index.shtml.

5 "Screening Tools," SAMHSA-HRSA Center for Integrated Health Solutions, accessed June 7, 2019. https://www.integration.samhsa.gov/clinical-practice/screening-tools.

6 "Instrument: Patient Health Questionnaire-2 (PHQ-2)," National Institute on Drug Abuse (NIDA) Clinical Trials Network (CTN)-recommended Common Data Elements (CDEs), accessed June 7, 2019, https://cde.drugabuse.gov/instrument/fc216f70-be8e-ac44-e040-bb89ad433387.

7 "Instrument: Patient Health Questionnaire-9 (PHQ-9)," National Institute on Drug Abuse (NIDA) Clinical Trials Network (CTN)-recommended Common Data Elements (CDEs), accessed June 7, 2019, https://cde.drugabuse.gov/instrument/f226b1a0-897c-de2a-e040-bb89ad4338b9.

8 "CAGE AID," Stable Resource Kit, Substance Abuse and Mental Health Services Administration (SAMHSA), U.S. Department of Health and Human Services, accessed June 7, 2019, https://www.integration.samhsa.gov/images/res/CAGEAID.pdf.

9 "AUDIT-C," Stable Resource Kit, Substance Abuse and Mental Health Services Administration (SAMHSA), U.S. Department of Health and Human Services, accessed June 7, 2019, https://www.integration.samhsa.gov/images/res/tool_auditc.pdf.

10 "AUDIT," Stable Resource Kit, Substance Abuse and Mental Health Services Administration (SAMHSA), U.S. Department of Health and Human Services, accessed June 7, 2019, https://www.integration.samhsa.gov/AUDIT_screener_for_alcohol.pdf.

11 "DAST-10 Questionnaire," Stable Resource Kit, Substance Abuse and Mental Health Services Administration (SAMHSA), U.S. Department of Health and Human Services, accessed June 7, 2019, http://www.emcdda.europa.eu/attachements.cfm/att_61480_EN_DAST%202008.pdf.

12 "SBIRT," Stable Resource Kit, Substance Abuse and Mental Health Services Administration (SAMHSA), U.S. Department of Health and Human Services, accessed June 7, 2019, https://www.integration.samhsa.gov/clinical-practice/sbirt.

13 Rhonda Livingstone, "What Does It Mean to Be Culturally Competent?" Refugee Assistance Program Workers, accessed June 7, 2019, http://rapworkers. com/wp-content/uploads/2017/08/what-does-it-mean-to-be-culturally-competent-1.pdf.

14 Edgar H. Schein, *Organizational Culture and Leadership*, (San Francisco: Jossey-Bass Publishers, 1992).

15 "Understanding Cultural Competency," Human Services Guide, HumanServicesEdu.org, accessed June 7, 2019, https://www.humanservicesedu. org/cultural-competency.html.

16 Kazuhiro Waza, et al., "Comparison of Symptoms in Japanese and American Depressed Primary Care Patients," *Family Practice*, October 1999, https://doi. org/10.1093/fampra/16.5.528.

17 Ibid.

18 "National Standards for Culturally And Linguistically Appropriate Services (CLAS) in Health and Health Care," U.S. Department of Health and Human Services, accessed June 7, 2019, https://www.thinkculturalhealth.hhs.gov/clas.

Chapter 6: Identifying the Biggest Opportunities to Deliver Value

1 "LACE tool," Michigan Care Management Resource Center (MiCRMC), accessed June 7, 2019. https://micmrc.org/system/files/LACE_tool%204.23.13.pdf.

2 Nate Moore, *Even Better Data, Better Decisions*, Medical Group Management Association, 2016.

3 "Health Information Technology Toolkit for Physician Offices," Stratis Health, accessed June 7, 2019, http://www.stratishealth.org/expertise/healthit/ clinics/clinictoolkit.html.

4 Wellness Recovery Action Plan® (WRAP®), Advocates for Human Potential, Inc., accessed June 7, 2019, https://mentalhealthrecovery.com/wrap-is/.

Chapter 7: Structuring the Practice

1 "Healthy People 2020," Office of Disease Prevention and Health Promotion (ODPHP), U.S. Department of Health and Human Services (HHS), accessed June 7, 2019, https://www.healthypeople.gov/.

2 "Healthcare Effectiveness Data and Information Set (HEDIS) and Performance Measurement," National Committee for Quality Assurance (NCQA), accessed June 7, 2019, https://www.ncqa.org/hedis/.

3 "Shared Decision-Making Implementation Roadmap," Minnesota Shared Decision-Making Collaborative, accessed June 7, 2019, http://msdmc.org/pdf/ MSDMCRoadmap.pdf.

Chapter 8: Incorporating Team-Based Care

1 Nick Fabrizio, "Overcoming Recruiting Challenges for Non-Clinical Staff," MGMA Stat, Medical Group Management Association (MGMA), accessed June 7, 2019, https://www.mgma.com/data/data-stories/overcoming-recruiting-challenges-for-non-clinical.

2 "The High Cost of Nurse Turnover," RNBSOnline, University of New Mexico, November 30, 2016, https://rnbsnonline.unm.edu/articles/high-cost-of-nurse-turnover.aspx.

3 "How Much Is Physician Turnover Really Costing You?" *Fierce Healthcare*, April 4, 2011, https://www.fiercehealthcare.com/healthcare/how-much-physician-turnover-really-costing-you.

4 David A. Frenz, "The Staggering Costs of Physician Turnover," *Today's Hospitalist*, Society of Hospital Medicine, accessed August 2016, https://www.todayshospitalist.com/staggering-costs-physician-turnover/.

5 Graham Mann, "What's the Real Cost of Employee Turnover?" *Optimization Blog*, Lean Systems, Inc., December 1, 2017, https://www.leansystems.co/blog/2017/12/1/cost-of-employee-turnover.

6 "Increase Physician Wellness & Reduce Burnout," *American Academy of Family Physicians*, accessed June 7, 2019, https://www.aafp.org/membership/benefits/physician-health-first.html.

7 Eva S. Schernhammer and Graham A. Colditz, "Suicide Rates Among Physicians: a Quantitative and Gender Assessment (Meta-Analysis)," *The American Journal of Psychiatry*, December 2004, https://www.ncbi.nlm.nih.gov/pubmed/15569903, DOI: 10.1176/appi.ajp.161.12.2295.

8 "Healthcare Professional Burnout, Depression and Suicide Prevention," American Foundation for Suicide Prevention (AFSP), accessed June 7, 2019,

https://afsp.org/our-work/education/healthcare-professional-burnout-depression-suicide-prevention/.

9 "Improving Care Through Teamwork," Primary Care Team Guide, Improving Primary Care, accessed June 7, 2019, http://www.improvingprimarycare.org/work/improving-care-through-teamwork

10 "Smart Goals – How to Make Your Goals Achievable," Mind Tools, accessed June 7, 2019, https://www.mindtools.com/pages/article/smart-goals.htm.

11 "Evaluating Team Effectiveness in a Primary Health Care Team," The Clinical Learning and Interprofessional Practice (CLIPP) unit, Saskatchewan Academic Health Sciences Network, accessed June 7, 2019, https://clippunit.ca/documents/ToolD_SCHRTeamEffectivenessToolJuly2011.pdf. This tool was developed using content from the Team Effectiveness Tool (Saskatchewan Health Primary Health Services Branch, 2002) and the Community Capacity Building Tool (Public Health Agency of Canada, 2007).

12 Bita A. Kash, et al., "Measuring Team Effectiveness in the Health Care Setting: An Inventory of Survey Tools," Health Services Insights, National Center for Biotechnology Information, U.S. National Library of Medicine, accessed August 24, 2018, doi:10.1177/1178632918796230, https://www.ncbi.nlm.nih.gov/pmc/articles/PMC6109848/.

13 "NICHQ's Care Plan Template," National Institute for Children's Health Quality (NICHQ), accessed June 7, 2019, https://www.nichq.org/resource/nichqs-care-plan-template.

14 "Build the Team," *Primary Care Team Guide,* Improving Primary Care, accessed June 7, 2019, http://www.improvingprimarycare.org/team.

15 "The Practice Team," *Primary Care Team Guide,* Improving Primary Care, accessed June 7, 2019, http://www.improvingprimarycare.org/team/practice-team

16 Lynda Gratton and Tamara J. Erickson, "Eight Ways to Build Collaborative Teams," *Harvard Business Review,* November 15, 2016, https://hbr.org/2007/11/eight-ways-to-build-collaborative-teams.

17 "Establishing the Care Team: Roles and Communications Toolkit," Stratis Health and KHA Health, with support from The Office of the National Coordinator for Health Information Technology (ONC), updated December 31, 2014, https://www.stratishealth.org/documents/

HITToolkitcoordination/3-Establishing-the-Care-Team-Roles-and-Communications.pdf.

18 Deborah Peikes, et al., "Primary Care Practice Facilitation Curriculum," *AHRQ Publication No. 15-0060-EF*, Agency for Healthcare Research and Quality (AHRQ), September 2015, https://pcmh.ahrq.gov/page/primary-care-practice-facilitation-curriculum.

19 Bruce W. Tuckman, "Developmental Sequence in Small Groups," *Psychological Bulletin,* July 1965, Doi:10.1037/h0022100, https://psycnet.apa.org/record/1965-12187-001. This is the article that introduced Tuckman's "forming, storming, norming, and performing" developmental process for groups.

20 "AHRQ Health Literacy Universal Precautions Toolkit, 2nd Edition," Agency for Healthcare Research and Quality (AHRQ), content last reviewed August 2018, https://www.ahrq.gov/professionals/quality-patient-safety/quality-resources/tools/literacy-toolkit/index.html.

21 Michelle O'Daniel and Alan H. Rosenstein, "Chapter 33 Professional Communication and Team Collaboration," in *Patient Safety and Quality: An Evidence-Based Handbook for Nurses,* ed. RG Hughes, Agency for Healthcare Research and Quality (AHRQ), April 2008, https://www.ncbi.nlm.nih.gov/books/NBK2637/.

22 Michael Zimmerman, "Planned Care Huddle," published March 18, 2008, video, 3:25, https://www.youtube.com/watch?v=Wttxm7jAnb4.

23 "Improving Care Through Teamwork," *Primary Care Team Guide,* Improving Primary Care, accessed June 9, 2019, http://www.improvingprimarycare.org/work/improving-care-through-teamwork.

24 Daniel P. Marlowe, et al., "A Team-Building Model for Team-Based Care." *Family Practice Management (FPM).* American Academy of Family Physicians. November-December 2012, https://www.aafp.org/fpm/2012/1100/p19.html.

Chapter 9: Being a Part of The Community and Involving the Medical Neighborhood

1 "Wraparound Basics or What Is Wraparound: An Introduction," National Wraparound Initiative, Regional Research Institute, School of Social Work,

Portland State University, accessed June 7, 2019, https://nwi.pdx.edu/wraparound-basics/.

2 Kathryn M. McDonald, et al., *Closing the Quality Gap: A Critical Analysis of Quality Improvement Strategies (Vol. 7: Care Coordination)*, Technical Review 9, Agency for Healthcare Research and Quality (AHRQ), June 2007, available at https://www.ncbi.nlm.nih.gov/books/NBK44015/.

3 Dhruv Khullar and Dave A. Chokshi, "Can Better Care Coordination Lower Health Care Costs?" *JAMA Network Open*, American Medical Association (AMA), November 2, 2018, doi:10.1001/jamanetworkopen.2018.4295, https://jamanetwork.com/journals/jamanetworkopen/fullarticle/2712173.

4 "Care Coordination Services Deliver Impressive Cost Saving Results,S" *eQHealth Blog*, January 26, 2017, https://www.eqhs.org/Resources/Blog/ID/85/Care-Coordination-Services-Deliver-Impressive-Cost-Saving-Results.

5 Naveen Rao, "Does Care Coordination Really Save Money? Does That Really Matter?" *Tincture*, May 24, 2017, https://tincture.io/does-care-coordination-really-save-money-does-that-really-matter-67da657f336e.

6 Eric A. Coleman, et al., "The Care Transitions Intervention: Results of a Randomized Controlled Trial," *Archives of Internal Medicine*, September 26, 2006, Doi:10.1001/archinte.166.17.1822, https://jamanetwork.com/journals/jamainternalmedicine/fullarticle/410933.

7 *Mental Health and Chronic Issues, Issue Brief No. 2,* National Healthy Workforce, Centers for Disease Control (CDC), October 2012, https://www.cdc.gov/workplacehealthpromotion/tools-resources/pdfs/issue-brief-no-2-mental-health-and-chronic-disease.pdf.

8 Ibid.

9 "Major Depression: The Impact on Overall Health," BlueCross BlueShield, May 10, 2018, https://www.bcbs.com/the-health-of-america/reports/major-depression-the-impact-overall-health.

10 Martha C. Ward, et al., "The Role of Behavioral Health in Optimizing Care for Complex Patients in the Primary Care Setting," *Journal of General Internal Medicine*, August 26, 2015, https://www.ncbi.nlm.nih.gov/pmc/articles/PMC4762832/.

11 "Managing Managed Care: Quality Improvement in Behavioral Health," Institute of Medicine (US) Committee on Quality Assurance and Accreditation Guidelines for Managed Behavioral Health Care; M Edmunds, et al., editors, January 1, 1997, https://www.ncbi.nlm.nih.gov/books/NBK233224/.

12 Kaitlynn Ely, "Behavioral Health Home Plus Model Has Positive Effects on Patients with Mental Illness," *The American Journal of Managed Care (AJMC)*, AJMC Managed Markets Network, February 20, 2018, https://www.ajmc.com/newsroom/behavioral-health-home-plus-model-has-positive-effects-on-patients-with-mental-illness.

13 Jessica Kent, "Behavioral Health Homes Boost Patient Engagement, Self-Management," *Health IT Analytics*, March 20, 2018, https://healthitanalytics.com/news/behavioral-health-homes-boost-patient-engagement-self-management.

14 "Statistics: Suicide," National Institute of Mental Health (NIMH), April 2019, https://www.nimh.nih.gov/health/statistics/suicide.shtml.

15 Lena H. Sun, "Why It's So Hard to Find a Mental Health Professional?" *The Washington Post*, October 22, 2015, https://www.washingtonpost.com/news/to-your-health/wp/2015/10/22/why-its-so-hard-to-find-a-mental-health-professional/.

16 Bruce Japsen, "Doctor Wait Times Soar 30% in Major U.S. Cities." *Forbes.com,* May 19, 2017, https://www.forbes.com/sites/brucejapsen/2017/03/19/doctor-wait-times-soar-amid-trumpcare-debate/#2c3634212e74.

17 Martha Gerrity, "Evolving Models of Behavioral Health Integration: Evidence Update 2010-2015," Milbank Memorial Fund, May 2016, https://www.milbank.org/wp-content/uploads/2016/05/Evolving-Models-of-BHI.pdf.

18 "Co-Location Of Services Model - Rural Services Integration Toolkit," Rural Health Information Hub (RHIhub), accessed June 7, 2019, https://www.ruralhealthinfo.org/toolkits/services-integration/2/co-location.

19 Flo Stein, "Co-Location of Behavioral Health and Primary Care Services: Community Care of North Carolina and The Center of Excellence for Integrated Care," *North Carolina Medical Journal*, January-February 2011, https://www.ncbi.nlm.nih.gov/pubmed/21678691.

20 Mark Moran, "Collaborative Care Found to Be Superior to Co-located Psychiatric Care," *Psychiatrics News*, American Psychiatric Association, September 18, 2018, https://psychnews.psychiatryonline.org/doi/full/10.1176/appi.pn.2018.9b15.

21 "Co-Location Is Not Enough," AIMS Center, Psychiatry and Behavioral Sciences Division of Population Health, University of Washington, accessed June 7, 2019, https://aims.uw.edu/co-location-not-enough.

22 David E. Goodrich, "Mental Health Collaborative Care and Its Role in Primary Care Settings," *Current Psychiatry Reports*, August 15, 2013, doi:10.1007/s11920-013-0383-2.

23 "IMPACT: Improving Mood—Promoting Access to Collaborative Treatment," AIMS Center, Psychiatry and Behavioral Sciences Division of Population Health, University of Washington, accessed June 7, 2019, http://aims.uw.edu/impact-improving-mood-promoting-access-collaborative-treatment/.

24 Steven K. Dobscha, et al., "Collaborative Care for Chronic Pain in Primary Care: A Cluster Randomized Trial," *Journal of the American Medical Association (JAMA)*, March 25, 2009, doi: 10.1001/jama.2009.377, https://jamanetwork.com/journals/jama/fullarticle/183624.

25 Peter Roy-Byrne, et al., "Delivery of Evidence-Based Treatment for Multiple Anxiety Disorders in Primary Care: A Randomized Controlled Trial." *Journal of the American Medical Association (JAMA)*, doi:10.1001/jama.2010.608, https://jamanetwork.com/journals/jama/fullarticle/185888.

26 Ya-Fen Chan, et al., "Substance Screening and Referral for Substance Abuse Treatment in an Integrated Mental Health Care Program," *Psychiatric Services*, January 2013, https://doi.org/10.1176/appi.ps.201200082, https://ps.psychiatryonline.org/doi/full/10.1176/appi.ps.201200082?url_ver=Z39.88-2003&rfr_id=ori:rid:crossref.org&rfr_dat=cr_pub%3dpubmed.

27 Martha Ward and Benjamin Druss, "Reverse Integration Initiatives for Individuals with Serious Mental Illness," *Focus*, July 18, 2017, https://doi.org/10.1176/appi.focus.20170011, https://focus.psychiatryonline.org/doi/abs/10.1176/appi.focus.20170011.

28 Alexandros Maragakis, et al., "Creating A 'Reverse' Integrated Primary and Mental Healthcare Clinic for Those with Serious Mental Illness," *Primary

Health Care Research & Development, November 20, 2015, https://www.cambridge.org/core/journals/primary-health-care-research-and-development/article/creating-a-reverse-integrated-primary-and-mental-healthcare-clinic-for-those-with-serious-mental-illness/283A715D47F6F28431D9E38E15AC1FB3#.

29 "Certified Community Behavioral Health Clinics (CCBHC)," National Council for Behavioral Heath, accessed June 7, 2019, https://www.thenationalcouncil.org/topics/certified-community-behavioral-health-clinics/.

30 "FY 2018 Certified Community Behavioral Health Clinic Expansion Grants," Substance Abuse and Mental Health Services Administration (SAMHSA), U.S. Department of Health and Human Services, updated December 19, 2018, https://www.samhsa.gov/grants/grant-announcements/sm-18-019.

31 "Integrating Behavioral Health into Primary Care: Lessons Learned from the Comprehensive Primary Care Initiative," TMF Health Quality Institute, July 2017, https://www.tmf.org/LinkClick.aspx?fileticket=gSv9OHvF_W8%3D&tabid=271&portalid=0&mid=741&forcedownload=true (download link).

32 "Implementation Quick Start Guide: Warm Handoff," *The Guide to Improving Patient Safety in Primary Care Settings by Engaging Patients and Families*, Agency for Healthcare Research and Quality (AHRQ), October 2, 2017, https://www.ahrq.gov/sites/default/files/wysiwyg/professionals/quality-patient-safety/patient-family-engagement/pfeprimarycare/warm-handoff-qsg-brochure.pdf.

33 "Analyzing the Costs of Integrated Care: A Brief Guide for SAMHSA PBHCI Grantees," SAMHSA-HRSA Center for Integrated Health Solutions. December 5, 2014, https://www.samhsa.gov/sites/default/files/programs_campaigns/samhsa_hrsa/integrated-care-cost-analysis.pdf.

34 Natasha B. Gouge, "An Economic Evaluation of Primary Care Behavioral Health in Pediatrics: A Case Study" (2013), Electronic Theses and Dissertations, Paper 1209, https://dc.etsu.edu/etd/1209, https://dc.etsu.edu/cgi/viewcontent.cgi?article=2370&context=etd.

35 "Integrating Primary Care and Behavioral Health Services: A Compass and A Horizon," Bureau of Primary Health Care Managed Care Technical Assistance Program, APA.org (American Psychological Association),

December 1, 2004, https://www.apa.org/practice/programs/rural/integrating-primary-behavioral.pdf.

Chapter 10: Involving the Patient

1 Adrienne Boissy, "Patient Engagement Vs. Patient Experience." *NEJM Catalyst*, Massachusetts Medical Society, December 28, 2018, https://catalyst.nejm.org/patient-engagement-vs-patient-experience/.

2 "What Is Patient Experience?" Agency for Healthcare Research and Quality (AHRQ), October 12, 2016, https://www.ahrq.gov/cahps/about-cahps/patient-experience/index.html.

3 "Consumer Assessment of Healthcare Providers and Systems (CAHPS) Surveys and Tools to Advance Patient-Centered Care," Agency for Healthcare Research and Quality (AHRQ), February 18, 2016, https://www.ahrq.gov/cahps/index.html.

4 Kate Niehous, "A Patient and Family Advisory Council for Quality: Making Its Voice Heard at Memorial Sloan Kettering Cancer Center," *NEJM Catalyst*, Memorial Sloan Kettering Cancer Center, December 7, 2016, https://catalyst.nejm.org/pfac-quality-memorial-sloan-kettering/.

5 Marie Ennis-O'Connor, "Patient Family Advisory Councils: What They Are, How They Help," *Patients Helping Patients Blog*, Patient Empowerment Network. September 15, 2014, https://powerfulpatients.org/2014/09/15/patient-family-advisory-councils-what-they-are-how-they-help/.

6 James O. Prochaska and Wayne F. Velicer, "The Transtheoretical Model of Health Behavior Change," *American Journal of Health Promotion*, September 1, 1997, https://doi.org/10.4278/0890-1171-12.1.38, https://journals.sagepub.com/doi/abs/10.4278/0890-1171-12.1.38.

7 Philip L. Ritter and Kate Lorig, "The English and Spanish Self-Efficacy to Manage Chronic Disease Scale Measures Were Validated Using Multiple Studies," *Journal of Clinical Epidemiology (JCE)*, November 2014, https://doi.org/10.1016/j.jclinepi.2014.06.009, https://www.jclinepi.com/article/S0895-4356(14)00235-2/fulltext.

8 "Self-Efficacy for Managing Chronic Disease 6-item Scale," Self-Management Resource Center, March 28, 2017, https://www.selfmanagementresource.com/docs/pdfs/English_-_self-efficacy_for_managing_chronic_disease_6-item.pdf.

9 John Wasson, "About HowsYourHealth and Permission to use HowsYourHealth Tools," FNX Corp. and Trustees of Dartmouth College, accessed June 7, 2019, https://howsyourhealth.com/static/html/whereWhy.html.

10 Guendalina Graffigna, "Viewing Patient Engagement Through the Patient's Eyes: A Must for Real Healthcare Innovation," *Engaging Patients Blog*, engagingpatients.org, February 11, 2016, http://www.engagingpatients.org/best-practices-and-methodologies/viewing-patient-engagement-patients-eyes-must-real-healthcare-innovation/.

11 Gendalina Graffigna, "Measuring Patient Engagement: Development and Psychometric Properties of the Patient Health Engagement (PHE) Scale," *Frontiers in Psychology*, March 27, 2015, https://doi.org/10.3389/fpsyg.2015.00274, https://www.frontiersin.org/articles/10.3389/fpsyg.2015.00274/full.

12 "Patient Activation Measure® (PAM®)," Insignia Health, accessed June 7, 2019, https://www.insigniahealth.com/products/pam-survey.

13 "Impact of Communication in Healthcare," Institute for Healthcare Communication, July 2011, https://healthcarecomm.org/about-us/impact-of-communication-in-healthcare/.

14 "Keep It Simple and Specific (KISS)." ISixSigma, accessed June 7, 2019, https://www.isixsigma.com/dictionary/keep-it-simple-and-specific-kiss/.

15 "Quick Guide to Health Literacy Fact Sheet," Office of Disease Prevention and Health Promotion, U.S. Department of Health and Human Services (HHS), accessed June 7, 2019, https://health.gov/communication/literacy/quickguide/factsbasic.htm.

16 "Health Literacy Measurement Tools (Revised)," Agency for Healthcare Research and Quality (AHRQ), September 2016, https://www.ahrq.gov/professionals/quality-patient-safety/quality-resources/tools/literacy/index.html.

17 "Health Literacy Assessment Tools," Duke University Medical Center Library & Archives, August 24, 2018, https://guides.mclibrary.duke.edu/healthliteracy/assessment.

18 "AHRQ Health Literacy Universal Precautions Toolkit, 2nd Edition," Agency for Healthcare Research and Quality (AHRQ), content last reviewed

August 2018, https://www.ahrq.gov/professionals/quality-patient-safety/quality-resources/tools/literacy-toolkit/index.html.

19 "Shared Decision Making," Stratis Health, January 10, 2015, https://www.stratishealth.org/documents/HITToolkitcoordination/6-Shared-Decision-Making.pdf.

20 "Healthwise for Care Transformation," Healthwise, accessed June 7, 2019, http://www.informedmedicaldecisions.org/what-is-shared-decision-making/.

21 "Diabetes Medication Choice," Mayo Clinic Shared Decision-Making National Resource Center, Mayo Foundation for Medical Education and Research, accessed June 7, 2019, https://shareddecisions.mayoclinic.org/decision-aid-information/decision-aids-for-chronic-disease/diabetes-medication-management/.

22 "Depression Medication Choice," Mayo Clinic Shared Decision-Making National Resource Center, Mayo Foundation for Medical Education and Research, accessed June 7, 2019, https://shareddecisions.mayoclinic.org/decision-aid-information/decision-aids-for-chronic-disease/depression-medication-choice/.

23 "Mayo Clinic Shared Decision-Making National Resource Center." N.D. Mayo Clinic. Mayo Foundation for Medical Education and Research, accessed June 7, 2019, https://shareddecisions.mayoclinic.org/.

24 "Center for Shared Decision Making: Shared Decision Making Resources at The Dartmouth Institute," Dartmouth-Hitchcock, accessed June 7, 2019, https://med.dartmouth-hitchcock.org/csdm_toolkits.html.

25 Taya Irizarry, et al., "Patient Portals and Patient Engagement: A State of the Science Review," *Journal of Medical Internet Research,* June 23, 2015, doi: 10.2196/jmir.4255, https://www.ncbi.nlm.nih.gov/pmc/articles/PMC4526960/.

26 "What Is A Patient Portal?" HealthIT.gov, The Office of the National Coordinator for Health Information Technology (ONC), last reviewed September 29, 2017. https://www.healthit.gov/faq/what-patient-portal.

27 "Empower Your Patients with Health Records on iPhone," Apple, Inc., accessed June 11, 2019, https://www.apple.com/healthcare/health-records/.

28 "Patient Satisfaction," Healthgrades.com, accessed June 11 2019, https://www.healthgrades.com/quality/patient-satisfaction.

29 "Healthgrades and MGMA Release Analysis of 7 Million Patient Reviews; Reveals What Patients Say About Their Doctors," *BusinessWire*, March 28, 2018, https://www.businesswire.com/news/home/20180328005370/en/Healthgrades-MGMA-Release-Analysis-7-Million-Patient.

Chapter 11: Getting Reimbursed

1 Tricia Leddy, et al., 2016. "Value-Based Payments In Medicaid Managed Care: An Overview of State Approaches," Center for Health Care Strategies, February 22, 2016, https://www.chcs.org/media/VBP-Brief_022216_FINAL.pdf.

2 Doral Jacobsen, and Nancy Robertson, *Transitioning to Alternative Payment Models: A Guide to Next Generation Managed Care Contracting*, Medical Group Management Association, 2017.

3 Thomas Beaton, "Humana Launches Bundled Payment Model for Maternity Care," *Healthpayer Intelligence*, April 23, 2018, https://healthpayerintelligence.com/news/humana-launches-bundled-payment-model-for-maternity-care.

4 "Alternative Payment Model, APM Framework," Health Care Payment Learning & Action Network (HCP-LAN), July 10, 2017, http://hcp-lan.org/workproducts/apm-refresh-whitepaper-final.pdf.

5 Ibid.

6 Laura Joszt "Payments Are Increasingly Tied to Value, But More Risk-Based Models Needed," *AJMC Managed Markets Network*, October 22, 2018, https://www.ajmc.com/newsroom/payments-are-increasingly-tied-to-value-but-more-riskbased-models-needed.

7 "Work RVU Calculator (Relative Value Units)," AAPC, accessed June 11, 2019, https://www.aapc.com/practice-management/rvu-calculator.aspx.

8 Todd Pickard, "Calculating Your Worth: Understanding Productivity and Value," *Journal of the Advanced Practitioner in Oncology*, March 1, 2014, https://www.ncbi.nlm.nih.gov/pmc/articles/PMC4093517/.

9 "Healthcare Effectiveness Data and Information Set (HEDIS) and Performance Measurement," National Committee for Quality Assurance (NCQA), accessed June 7, 2019, https://www.ncqa.org/hedis/.

10 "Health Plan Ratings Results," National Committee for Quality Assurance (NCQA), accessed June 11, 2019, http://healthinsuranceratings.ncqa.org.

Chapter 12: Keeping the Momentum

1 *Crossing the Quality Chasm: A New Health System for the 21st Century,* Institute of Medicine (US) Committee on Quality of Health Care in America, National Academies Press (US), Vol 2, *Improving the 21st-century Health Care System*, accessed June 6, 2019, available from: https://www.ncbi.nlm.nih.gov/books/NBK222265/.

2 Mark R. Chassin, et al., "The Urgent Need to Improve Health Care Quality: Consensus Statement" Institute of Medicine National Roundtable on Health Care Quality, 1998, available at: https://www.ncbi.nlm.nih.gov/books/NBK223995/.

3 Cristina Boccuti and Giselle Casillas. "Aiming for Fewer Hospital U-turns: The Medicare Hospital Readmission Reduction Program," The Henry J. Kaiser Family Foundation, March 10, 2017, https://www.kff.org/medicare/issue-brief/aiming-for-fewer-hospital-u-turns-the-medicare-hospital-readmission-reduction-program/.

4 "The History of Six Sigma," iSixSigma.com, accessed June 11, 2019, https://www.isixsigma.com/new-to-six-sigma/history/history-six-sigma/.

5 Mark Crawford, "5 Lean Principles Every Engineer Should Know," The American Society of Mechanical Engineers (ASME), March 2016, https://www.asme.org/engineering-topics/articles/manufacturing-design/5-lean-principles-every-should-know.

6 "8 Wastes," The Basics of Lean Six Sigma (blog), GoLeanSixSigma.com, accessed June 11, 2019, https://goleansixsigma.com/8-wastes/.

7 Adam Henshall, "DMAIC: The Complete Guide to Lean Six Sigma in 5 Key Steps," Process Street, November 24, 2017, https://www.process.st/dmaic/.

8 "Quality Improvement Essentials Toolkit," Institute for Healthcare Improvement, accessed June 11, 2019, http://www.ihi.org/resources/Pages/Tools/Quality-Improvement-Essentials-Toolkit.aspx.

9 "How to Improve," Institute for Healthcare Improvement, June 11, 2019, http://www.ihi.org/resources/Pages/HowtoImprove/default.aspx.

About The Author

Jennifer Ternay is a healthcare expert that shares over two decades of knowledge to help healthcare organizations succeed despite the challenges and constant disruptions to the industry. Offering insights to solve problems with an approach that is founded in values, Jennifer offers strategic consulting to help healthcare organizations reduce healthcare costs, obtain healthier patient outcomes and improve patient experience. Blending financial and operational knowledge, she is passionate about the delivery of integrated, patient-centered care and assisting clients to meet the challenges of today's healthcare environment.

Jennifer's consulting career began in 2010 after working in public accounting and managed care. Prior to creating her consulting business, she was the CEO for a statewide Medicaid ASO program in Maryland with previous leadership positions as CFO. Jennifer's education and certifications include Bachelors in Business Administration (Accounting), Masters in Business Administration as well as licensure as a Certified Public Accountant (CPA) and NCQA recognition as a Patient-Centered Medical Home Certified Content Expert (PCMH CCE).

jennifer@valuesbasedcare.com

www.ingramcontent.com/pod-product-compliance
Lightning Source LLC
Chambersburg PA
CBHW061148220326
41599CB00025B/4395